~BodyMinder~
Workout & Exercise Journal

A Fitness Diary
by MemoryMinder Journals

"See your goals become reality!"

This journal belongs to

_____

_____

BodyMinder *Workout & Exercise Journal*
MemoryMinder Journals, Inc.
Copyright ©2002 by F. E. Wilkins
Periodic revisions

ISBN# 978-09637968-4-4
UPC 700703-81844-4

For information regarding this publication:
MemoryMinder Journals, Inc.
PO Box 23108
Eugene, OR 97402-0425
(541)342-2300
www.memoryminder.com

Made in the USA
bm15+eofw

What do you have to gain
from a regular exercise program?

- Increased self esteem
- More energy
- A stronger heart
- More calories and fat burned
- Lower cholesterol
- Stress relief
- Clearer thinking
- Increased metabolism
- Lowered risk of certain diseases
- Prevention of bone loss

In short, you'll look good and feel great!

The BodyMinder can be used with virtually any
fitness program or workout regimen.

~Other books by MemoryMinder Journals~

- **DietMinder**
Personal Food & Fitness Journal

- **HealthMinder**
Personal Wellness Journal

- **MaintenanceMinder**
Daily Weigh-In Journal

- **DietMinder JUNIOR**
*Food & Exercise Journal
for Kids 6 & Up*

~Table of Contents~

PART ONE
Information and Inspiration [cream pages]

- Introduction
- Tips for Using Your **BodyMinder**
  (with examples)
- Common Food Counts
- Calorie Expenditure Guide
- Heart Rate and Blood Pressure Ranges

PART TWO
Weekly and Daily Records [white pages]

- Weekly Plans
- Daily Activity (91 days)

PART THREE
Additional Records [cream pages]

- Health Clubs/Gyms
- Starting Statistics and Goals
- Weekly Progress
- Games & Competitions
- Fitness Expenses
- Reorder Form

- Vinyl Utility Pocket

~Introduction~

The BodyMinder Workout & Exercise Journal was designed to help you keep track of all things physical...from pumping iron to ironing your clothes! Wherever you exercise (gym, home, etc.) and whatever you do, there's a place to record it in this journal.

Experts agree that along with physical activity, a healthy diet is essential. With that in mind, the BodyMinder also provides space to record your day's food and supplement intake.

Why keep a journal? Time and again it's been proven that writing things down can help you be more organized, focused, and committed to your goals. When you see your efforts in black and white, you'll be better able to analyze progress and detect areas that may need improvement.

Using apps or other fitness devices can also be beneficial. The BodyMinder is "app friendly" so you can easily transfer those counts onto your daily journal pages to encompass even more information about your progress.

If you're starting a new fitness plan or workout regimen, record-keeping can be especially important to keep you on track in a safe and healthy way. As time passes, using your journal will continue to help keep you motivated. It really does work!

As you fill the pages of your BodyMinder, a personal memoir of an important achievement will be created...your journey to a healthier body and lifestyle. In addition, your Journal will provide details for future reference and an overall picture of what works best for you.

The BodyMinder does not make suggestions or recommendations about how much or what kind of exercise you need; that's the role of your trainer or physical fitness expert. We do recommend that you discuss your plan with a professional before starting any vigorous regimen. A checkup with your doctor is also a good idea.

As with all our journals, please feel free to contact us if you have any suggestions for additions or changes to this book. We truly enjoy hearing from you and take every comment and suggestion seriously.

Tips for Using Your
~BodyMinder~

The BodyMinder has room for thirteen weeks (91 days) of journaling. However, since the pages are not predated, it can be used daily or intermittently and thus, may last even longer.

To make your Journal easier to use, it's divided into three sections. The front cream-colored pages contain tips and information such as "Common Food Counts" (which can be customized by adding your own favorite foods). The white pages, the heart of the Journal, are for your weekly plans and daily activities. The back cream-colored section has room for additional fitness-related records.

1. **Starting Stats and Goals...**(*located in the back*) On this page you can list your current measurements and other facts. Next to that, list the goals you would like to reach over the next thirteen weeks. Be realistic...pick goals that are challenging yet attainable in the given amount of time.

2. **Weekly Plans...**(*beginning of white pages*) Now that you have your goals in mind, a written plan of action is a good idea. In the upper half of

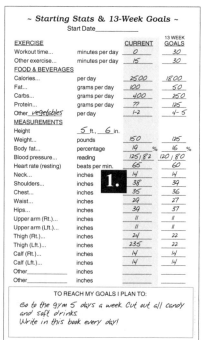

Starting Stats & 13-week Goals

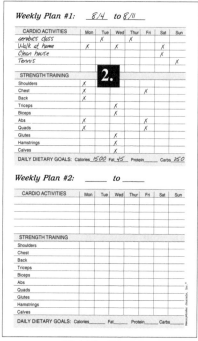

Weekly Plans

each weekly planning area, list the cardio exercises you intend to do in the coming week and put an "x" in each box on the day you plan to do them. In the "strength training" area simply mark the days based upon the specific muscle groups on which you plan to focus. A new schedule can be made each week using your previous week's results and performance as a guide. There's also room for dietary goals.

3. **Daily Workouts...** Each "day" consists of two pages. The left-hand page focuses on activities generally done in a gym or fitness center. You can record both cardio and strength training details here such as the time spent, heart rate, number of calories burned, area of focus, reps & sets, equipment weight or setting, muscle groups, and level of difficulty.

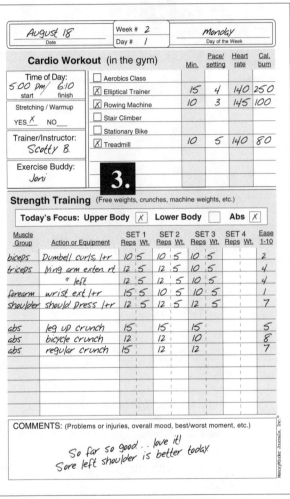

Daily Activity, left-hand page

In addition, you can list the time you worked out, your trainer, workout partner, and comments such as mood, injuries, tips, etc. Try to keep accurate records, especially in the first few weeks. This will get you off to a good start and help you form good habits. It can also provide insight for adjusting your regimen as you progress.

Daily Activity, right-hand page

Other Exercise (outside the gym)

Activity	Hrs./Min./Qty.	Intensity (Low Med. High)	Cal. Burn
Walked with Amy & Kayla (Steps on walk = 8142)	90 min.	x	540
Raked leaves in front	1 hr.	x	400
vacuumed downstairs	30 min	x	150

4.

Dietary Notes — CALORIES / FAT GMS / CARBS / PROTEIN

	CALORIES	FAT GMS	CARBS	PROTEIN
Breakfast				
1 c. oatmeal	145	2	25	6
6 oz. OJ	65		16	
1 toast	70	1	12	3
1 T Jelly	51		12	
Snack				
energy bar	280	4	30	12
Lunch				
6 Walnut halves	80	8	2	3
apple	81		21	
diet coke				
Snack				
1 Nectarine	67		16	1
Dinner				
6 oz. Chicken breast	300	8		45
Broccoli	12		2	1
1 c. Rice	160		38	3
Salad	20		2	1
2T dressing	150	20		
Snack				
1/4 c. raisins	125		33	1
GRAND TOTALS...	1606	42	209	65

Water (8 oz. glasses)
X X X X X
X X ☐ ☐ ☐

Vitamins, Supplements

NAME / STRENGTH	QTY.
multi vit	2
Calcium 500	3
vit E, 400iu	1
vit c	1
Lipitor	1

5. OTHER NOTES

Get vitamin E and batteries!

*meet Danny & Rob on Fri.

TOTAL STEPS TODAY = 10,452

Met todays goals?
0%   25%   50%   75%   100%   X

MemoryMinder Journals, Inc. ©

---

4.   **Other Exercise...** In the upper half of the right-hand daily page, you can make note of any other exercise you did today such as swimming, walking, running, biking, gardening, dancing, golfing, etc. (Don't forget housework!) Time or distance, intensity, and calories burned can be noted, too.

5.   **Dietary Notes & More...** If you're on a special diet or simply watching what you eat, here is space to record your meals, food counts, water, vitamins and supplements.

If your fitness plan calls for 5-6 meals per day, the snack areas can be utilized. At the end of each day add up your totals and mark the bar in the bottom corner with the percentage by which you feel you reached your daily goals.

Reminders, notes, or readings from any fitness device such as a pedometer or other tracking system can be posted, too. Record this info in the **Other Notes** area or wherever appropriate on the daily pages.

6.   **Healthclub information...** *(not pictured)* In the back cream-colored section of the BodyMinder, the first page contains space for information about the club(s) to which you belong and your membership details.

~Weekly Progress~

	Week 1 8/10 Date	Week 2 8/17 Date	Week 3 Date
Weight	148	146	
Body fat			
Blood pressure	124/82	124/81	
Heart rate (RESTING)	65	65	
Neck		14	
Shoulders		38	
Chest		35	
Waist	28.5	28	
Hips		38	
Upper arm (Rt.)		11	
Upper arm (Lft.)		11	
Thigh (Rt.)		23	
Thigh (Lft.)		23	
Calf (Rt.)		14	
Calf (Lft.)		14	

	Week 4 Date	Week 5 Date	Week 6 Date
Weight			
Body fat			
Blood pressure			
Heart rate (RESTING)			
Neck			
Shoulders			
Chest			
Waist			
Hips			
Upper arm (Rt.)			
Upper arm (Lft.)			
Thigh (Rt.)			
Thigh (Lft.)			
Calf (Rt.)			
Calf (Lft.)			

Weekly Progress

7. **Weekly Progress...** When all is said and done, filling out these pages may be the part you find most rewarding! Keeping a progress chart can definitely keep you motivated and on top of your game.

8. **Games & Competitions...** Satisfy your competitive urges by keeping track of any games, track meets, body building competitions or other sports in which you participate. There are several pages to list dates, locations, participants, and scores.

~Games & Competitions~

Date	Event & Location	Participants	Result/Score
May 4	Butte to Butte 10K run Eugene	half the town!	I came in 34/21 Yes!
June 27	Golf at Creswell 9 holes beautiful day!	Danny, Pauline Scott & me	D- 50 P- 47 R- 51 me- 46.111
June 30	Ping Pong tourney	Club members	I came in 5th out of 17
July 14	Golf at Creswell 18 holes	Dan, me WE TIED!	D- 101 me- 101
July 16	Softball at McClure Field	Ducks vs Bulldogs GO DUCKS!	them- 3 us- 7

Games & Competitions

9. **Fitness Expenses...** "What is all this costing me?" Maybe you don't really want to know...but for those who like to see the dollars and "sense" of things, here's a place to list and categorize fitness expenses.

$ ~Fitness Expenses~ $

Athletic Clothing
Shoes, Shorts, Shirts, etc.

Date	Item	Amount Paid
May 1	2 Pr socks	$ 10-
June 27	Navy warm-up suit	$ 85-
July 1	Nike running shoes	$ 60-
July 30	Black leotard & tights	$ 55-
		$
		$
		$
		$
		$
		$
		$
		$
		$

Equipment Purchases
Weights, balls, racquets, clubs, etc.

Date	Item	Amount Paid
June 25	Putter	$ 45-
June 27	Golf balls (5)	$ 12-
July 29	Basketball (for Rob)	$ 20-
		$
		$
		$
		$
		$
		$
		$
		$
		$
		$

Fitness expenses

Last but not least... In the back you'll find a handy vinyl pocket for "before and after" photos, membership cards, schedules, receipts, notes, etc. Also a reorder form is provided in case BodyMinders are unavailable at stores in your area.

Remember, take your BodyMinder along wherever you go and use it faithfully. If you do, your commitment will stay strong and your goals will soon become reality. ***Good luck!***

~Common Food Counts~
(approximate)

~A~

Food	Amt.	Cal	Fat	Carbs	Prot.
Almonds	1oz	167	15	6	6
Apple, med.	1	81	.5	21	.3
Applesauce/swt.	½c	97	.2	26	.2
Applesauce/unswt	½c	53	.1	14	.2
Apricot/med.	3	51	.4	12	1.5
Artichoke/med.	1	60	.2	13	4
Avocado/med.	1	306	30	12	4

~B~

Food	Amt.	Cal	Fat	Carbs	Prot.
Bacon,fried	2pc.	70	6	5	0
Bagel, plain	1	150	1	34	9
Baked beans	½c	170	1	21	6
Banana, med.	1	105	.6	27	1
Beef, ground lean	4oz	308	21	0	28
Beef, T-bone	4 oz	243	12	0	32
Beer, regular	12oz	146	0	13	1
Blueberries,fresh	½c	41	.3	10	.5
Bread, wheat	1sl.	70	1	12	3
Broccoli,chopped	½c	12	.2	2	1
Burger, *Big Mac*	1	560	31	45	26
Burger, *Whopper*	1	640	39	45	27
Butter	1T	100	11	0	.1

~C~

Food	Amt.	Cal	Fat	Carbs	Prot.
Candy:					
M&M's, plain	¼c	210	9	30	2
Jelly bean, sm.	35	140	0	37	0
Cantalope cubes	½c	29	.2	7	.7
Carrot, whole 7"	1	30	.1	7	.7
Cashews, roastd	18	163	8	14	5
Celery, 7" stalk	1	6	.1	1	.3
Cheese, cheddar	1oz	110	9	1	7
Chicken-dark meat	4oz	232	11	0	31

Food	Amt.	Cal	Fat	Carbs	Prot.
Chicken-lightmeat	4oz	196	5	0	35
Chips, potato	15	160	10	14	2
Chips, corn	14	150	10	16	2
Coffee, brewed	6oz	4	0	1	.1
Cookie, *Oreo*	3	160	7	23	1
Corn, frozen	½c	80	1	17	2
Corn flakes	1oz	100	0	24	2
Cott. cheese/lofat	½c	100	2	4	14
Crackers, *Ritz*	5	80	4	10	1
Cream, 25%fat	1T	37	4	.5	.4

~D~

Food	Amt.	Cal	Fat	Carbs	Prot.
Dates, pitted	5	120	0	32	1
Dill pickle	1	13	0	3	.4
Donut, glazed	1	250	12	33	3

~E~

Food	Amt.	Cal	Fat	Carbs	Prot.
Eggs:					
Raw, large	1	75	5	.6	6
Raw, white only	1	17	0	.3	4
Boiled,chopped	1c	210	14	1.5	17
Eggplant,raw,chop	½c	11	.1	2.5	.4

~F~

Food	Amt.	Cal	Fat	Carbs	Prot.
Flatfish (sole,etc.)	4oz	104	1	0	21
Fries *McD's sm bag*	1	210	10	26	3
Franks,*O.Mayer*	1	150	13	1	5
Frosting, canned	2T	130	5	22	0

~G~

Food	Amt.	Cal	Fat	Carbs	Prot.
Grapes, seedless	10	36	.3	9	.3
Grapejuice	½c	80	0	20	0
Grapefruit, med.	½	46	.1	12	.6
Green beans, raw	½c	17	.1	4	1
Guacamole	2T	50	4	3	1

~H~

Food	Amt.	Cal	Fat	Carbs	Prot.
Halibut, baked	4oz	159	3	0	30
Ham, diced-lean	4oz	249	13	0	32
Honey	1T	60	0	16	0
Hummus	2T	50	4	5	2

~I~

Food	Amt.	Cal	Fat	Carbs	Prot.
Ice cream:					
Van. *Haagen Dazs*	½c	260	17	23	5
Dove Bar	1	280	19	23	5
Ice Milk, lo-fat	½c	100	2	17	3

~J~

Food	Amt.	Cal	Fat	Carbs	Prot.
Jam, *Smucker's*	1tsp	18	0	4	0
Jelly, *Welch's*	2tsp	35	0	9	0
Jicama, raw-cubed	½c	23	.1	5	.4

~K~

Food	Amt.	Cal	Fat	Carbs	Prot.
Kidney beans	½c	112	.4	20	8
Kielbasa	2oz	190	17	2	8
Kiwi, medium	1	46	.3	11	1

~L~

Food	Amt.	Cal	Fat	Carbs	Prot.
Lamb loin, lean	4oz	229	11	0	30
Lentils, dry	¼c	70	0	19	8
Lettuce, shred.	½c	5	.1	1	.4
Liver, beef-fried	4oz	246	9	9	30
Lobster	4oz	108	1	1	22

~M~

Food	Amt.	Cal	Fat	Carbs	Prot.
Mac&Chse/*Kraft*	1c	410	18	48	11
Maple Syrup	1T	50	0	13	0
Margarine	1T	100	11	0	0
Mayonnaise	1T	100	11	0	0
Milk, whole	1c	150	8	11	8
Milk, non-fat	1c	90	0	13	9
Muffin, English	1	132	1	29	5
Mushroom, raw	½c	9	.2	2	1
Mustard	1T	11	1	1	1

~N~

Food	Amt.	Cal	Fat	Carbs	Prot.
Nectarine, med.	1	67	.6	16	1
Noodles, egg cooked	1c	212	2	40	8
Nuts, mixed	1oz	175	16	6	5

~O~

Food	Amt.	Cal	Fat	Carbs	Prot.
Oatmeal, cooked	1c	145	2	25	6
Olive oil	1T	120	14	0	0
Onion, raw	½c	30	.1	7	1
Orange med.	1	65	.1	16	1
Orange juice	6oz	80	0	20	1
Oyster, raw, med	6	57	2	3	6

~PQ~

Food	Amt.	Cal	Fat	Carbs	Prot.
Pasta, cooked	1c	197	1	40	7
Peach, fresh	1	37	.1	10	1
Peanuts, oil roastd	1oz	163	14	5	7
Peanut butter	2T	188	16	7	8
Pear, fresh	1	98	1	25	1
Peas, fresh	½c	30	.1	5	2
Pepper, bell-med	1	20	.1	5	1
Pizza, pepperoni	1sl	253	10	28	20
Popcorn, plain	4c	130	6	16	3
Potato, baked	1	220	.2	51	5

~R~

Food	Amt.	Cal	Fat	Carbs	Prot.
Raisins, seedless	½c	250	0	66	3
Raspberry, fresh	½c	31	.3	7	1
Refried beans	½c	134	1.4	23	8
Rice, white,cooked	1c	160	.5	38	3
Rice, brn, cooked	1c	166	2	37	3

~S~

Food	Amt.	Cal	Fat	Carbs	Prot.
Salmon, baked	4oz	234	14	0	25
Salsa, red	2T	10	0	2	0
Sardines in oil	2	50	3	0	6
Sherbet	½c	130	1	28	1
Shrimp, large,raw	4	30	.5	.3	6
Softdrinks, reg.	12oz	144	0	38	0
Sour Cream	1T	26	2.5	.5	.4
Soy milk	1c	79	5	4	7
Strawberry, fresh	½c	23	.3	5	.5
Sugar, granulated	1tsp	15	0	4	0

~T~

Food	Amt.	Cal	Fat	Carbs	Prot.
Tofu, raw-firm	½c	183	11	5	20
Tomato, med.	1	26	.4	6	1
Tomato juice	6oz	32	.1	8	1
Tortilla, corn-sm.	1	40	.5	8	1
Tuna, canned/water	2oz	60	.5	0	12
Turkey, dark meat	4oz	212	8	0	32
Turkey, lt. meat	4oz	178	4	0	40

~UVW~

Food	Amt.	Cal	Fat	Carbs	Prot.
V-8 Veg. Juice	6 oz	35	0	8	1
Vienna sausage	1oz	69	7	2	3
Waffle, Eggo	1	120	5	16	3
Walnut halves	1c	642	62	18	14
Watermln-diced	½c	25	.3	6	.5
Wheat germ	1oz	103	3	12	9
Wine, dry, table	1oz	25	0	1	0

~XYZ~

Food	Amt.	Cal	Fat	Carbs	Prot.
Yams, baked	½c	79	.1	19	1
Yams, canned	½c	90	0	20	2
Yogurt, plain	1c	150	4	17	12
Yogurt, froz.van.	½c	110	3	19	3
Zucchini, raw	½c	9	.1	2	1

~Calorie Expenditure Guide~

The rate at which your body burns calories is determined by your weight and by the intensity of your physical activity. The more you weigh and/or the harder you work, the more calories you will burn per hour. True caloric expenditure can vary significantly from person to person.*

A general rule of thumb is this:
- Light exercise burns about 3-5 calories per minute
- Medium exercise burns about 6-8 calories per minute
- Heavy exercise burns about 9-11 calories per minute

In <u>one hour</u> these activities burn <u>roughly</u>:

250-350 calories	450-550 calories	650-850 calories
• slow walking	• brisk walking	• jogging
• light gardening	• swimming	• wrestling
• slow dancing	• basketball	• cross country skiing
• light housework	• bicycling	• football training
• ping pong, friendly	• aerobic dance	• raquetball, advanced
• tennis, doubles	• weight training	• jumping rope
• golf, social	• tennis, singles	• climbing stairs

* For more specific figures, do a key word search of "calories burned" on the internet. You'll find numerous sites where calorie counts can be calulated based upon your exact weight, activity, and time spent.

~ *Average Heart Rate Ranges**~

The following figures show estimates of the average heart rate (beats per minute-bpm) **during exercise**.

Age	Low	High
20	100 bpm	170 bpm
25	98 bpm	166 bpm
30	95 bpm	162 bpm
35	93 bpm	157 bpm
40	90 bpm	153 bpm
45	88 bpm	149 bpm
50	85 bpm	145 bpm
55	83 bpm	140 bpm
60	80 bpm	136 bpm

* Remember...these are estimates only...your own rate during exercise may be somewhat lower or higher. Before beginning any strenuous exercise program, be sure to consult your doctor and fitness professional.

~ *Average Blood Pressure Ranges**~

Rating	Systolic	Diastolic
Normal/low	below 130	below 85
Normal/high	130-139	85-89
Moderate	140-159	90-99
High	160-179	100-109
Very high	180+	110+

* Blood pressure readings can vary throughout one's lifetime and may also be influenced by various factors such as time of day and amount of activity. If you have repeated readings above the normal ranges, a visit to your doctor is advisable.

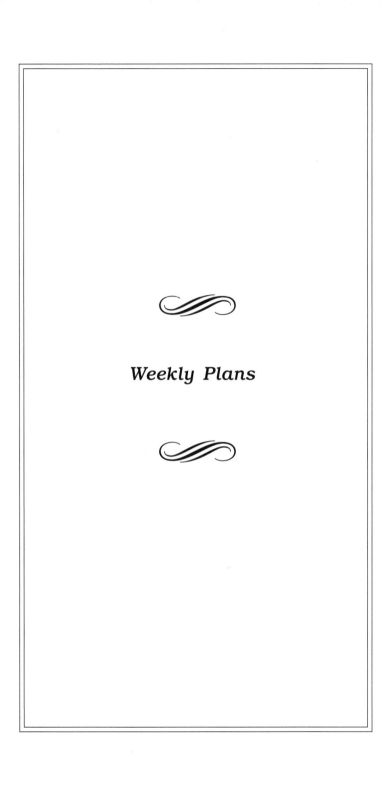

Weekly Plans

Weekly Plan #1: _____ *to* _____

CARDIO ACTIVITIES	Mon	Tue	Wed	Thur	Fri	Sat	Sun

STRENGTH TRAINING

	Mon	Tue	Wed	Thur	Fri	Sat	Sun
Shoulders							
Chest							
Back							
Triceps							
Biceps							
Abs							
Quads							
Glutes							
Hamstrings							
Calves							

DAILY DIETARY GOALS: Calories_____ Fat_____ Protein_____ Carbs_____

Weekly Plan #2: _____ *to* _____

CARDIO ACTIVITIES	Mon	Tue	Wed	Thur	Fri	Sat	Sun

STRENGTH TRAINING

	Mon	Tue	Wed	Thur	Fri	Sat	Sun
Shoulders							
Chest							
Back							
Triceps							
Biceps							
Abs							
Quads							
Glutes							
Hamstrings							
Calves							

DAILY DIETARY GOALS: Calories_____ Fat_____ Protein_____ Carbs_____

Weekly Plan #3: _____ to _____

CARDIO ACTIVITIES	Mon	Tue	Wed	Thur	Fri	Sat	Sun

STRENGTH TRAINING							
Shoulders							
Chest							
Back							
Triceps							
Biceps							
Abs							
Quads							
Glutes							
Hamstrings							
Calves							

DAILY DIETARY GOALS: Calories_____ Fat_____ Protein_____ Carbs_____

Weekly Plan #4: _____ to _____

CARDIO ACTIVITIES	Mon	Tue	Wed	Thur	Fri	Sat	Sun

STRENGTH TRAINING							
Shoulders							
Chest							
Back							
Triceps							
Biceps							
Abs							
Quads							
Glutes							
Hamstrings							
Calves							

DAILY DIETARY GOALS: Calories_____ Fat_____ Protein_____ Carbs_____

Weekly Plan #5: _____ *to* _____

CARDIO ACTIVITIES	Mon	Tue	Wed	Thur	Fri	Sat	Sun

STRENGTH TRAINING							
Shoulders							
Chest							
Back							
Triceps							
Biceps							
Abs							
Quads							
Glutes							
Hamstrings							
Calves							

DAILY DIETARY GOALS: Calories_____ Fat_____ Protein_____ Carbs_____

Weekly Plan #6: _____ *to* _____

CARDIO ACTIVITIES	Mon	Tue	Wed	Thur	Fri	Sat	Sun

STRENGTH TRAINING							
Shoulders							
Chest							
Back							
Triceps							
Biceps							
Abs							
Quads							
Glutes							
Hamstrings							
Calves							

DAILY DIETARY GOALS: Calories_____ Fat_____ Protein_____ Carbs_____

Weekly Plan #7: _____ to _____

CARDIO ACTIVITIES	Mon	Tue	Wed	Thur	Fri	Sat	Sun
STRENGTH TRAINING							
Shoulders							
Chest							
Back							
Triceps							
Biceps							
Abs							
Quads							
Glutes							
Hamstrings							
Calves							

DAILY DIETARY GOALS: Calories_____ Fat_____ Protein_____ Carbs_____

Weekly Plan #8: _____ to _____

CARDIO ACTIVITIES	Mon	Tue	Wed	Thur	Fri	Sat	Sun
STRENGTH TRAINING							
Shoulders							
Chest							
Back							
Triceps							
Biceps							
Abs							
Quads							
Glutes							
Hamstrings							
Calves							

DAILY DIETARY GOALS: Calories_____ Fat_____ Protein_____ Carbs_____

Weekly Plan #9: _____ to _____

CARDIO ACTIVITIES	Mon	Tue	Wed	Thur	Fri	Sat	Sun

STRENGTH TRAINING							
Shoulders							
Chest							
Back							
Triceps							
Biceps							
Abs							
Quads							
Glutes							
Hamstrings							
Calves							

DAILY DIETARY GOALS: Calories_____ Fat_____ Protein_____ Carbs_____

Weekly Plan #10: _____ to _____

CARDIO ACTIVITIES	Mon	Tue	Wed	Thur	Fri	Sat	Sun

STRENGTH TRAINING							
Shoulders							
Chest							
Back							
Triceps							
Biceps							
Abs							
Quads							
Glutes							
Hamstrings							
Calves							

DAILY DIETARY GOALS: Calories_____ Fat_____ Protein_____ Carbs_____

MemoryMinder Journals, Inc.©

Weekly Plan #11: _____ to _____

CARDIO ACTIVITIES	Mon	Tue	Wed	Thur	Fri	Sat	Sun

STRENGTH TRAINING							
Shoulders							
Chest							
Back							
Triceps							
Biceps							
Abs							
Quads							
Glutes							
Hamstrings							
Calves							

DAILY DIETARY GOALS: Calories_____ Fat_____ Protein_____ Carbs_____

Weekly Plan #12: _____ to _____

CARDIO ACTIVITIES	Mon	Tue	Wed	Thur	Fri	Sat	Sun

STRENGTH TRAINING							
Shoulders							
Chest							
Back							
Triceps							
Biceps							
Abs							
Quads							
Glutes							
Hamstrings							
Calves							

DAILY DIETARY GOALS: Calories_____ Fat_____ Protein_____ Carbs_____

MemoryMinder Journals, Inc.©

Weekly Plan #13: _____ *to* _____

CARDIO ACTIVITIES	Mon	Tue	Wed	Thur	Fri	Sat	Sun
STRENGTH TRAINING							
Shoulders							
Chest							
Back							
Triceps							
Biceps							
Abs							
Quads							
Glutes							
Hamstrings							
Calves							

DAILY DIETARY GOALS: Calories_____ Fat_____ Protein_____ Carbs_____

Daily Activity Records

Date	Week #	
	Day #	Day of the Week

Cardio Workout (in the gym)

	Min.	Pace/ setting	Heart rate	Cal. burn

Time of Day:

start / finish

Stretching / Warmup

YES___   NO___

Trainer/Instructor:

Exercise Buddy:

Exercise	Min.	Pace/ setting	Heart rate	Cal. burn
☐ Aerobics Class				
☐ Elliptical Trainer				
☐ Rowing Machine				
☐ Stair Climber				
☐ Stationary Bike				
☐ Treadmill				

Strength Training (Free weights, crunches, machine weights, etc.)

Today's Focus: Upper Body ☐   Lower Body ☐   Abs ☐

Muscle Group	Action or Equipment	SET 1 Reps	Wt.	SET 2 Reps	Wt.	SET 3 Reps	Wt.	SET 4 Reps	Wt.	Ease 1-10

COMMENTS: (Problems or injuries, overall mood, best/worst moment, etc.)

Other Exercise (outside the gym)

Activity	Hrs./Min./Qty.	Intensity	Cal. Burn
		Low Med. High	

Dietary Notes	CALORIES	FAT GMS	CARBS	PROTEIN
Breakfast				
Snack				
Lunch				
Snack				
Dinner				
Snack				
GRAND TOTALS...				

Water (8 oz. glasses)

☐ ☐ ☐ ☐ ☐
☐ ☐ ☐ ☐ ☐

Vitamins, Supplements
NAME / STRENGTH   QTY.

OTHER NOTES:

Met today's goals?
0%   25%   50%   75%   100%

Date	Week #	
	Day #	Day of the Week

Cardio Workout (in the gym)

	Min.	Pace/ setting	Heart rate	Cal. burn

Time of Day:					
start / finish	☐ Aerobics Class				
	☐ Elliptical Trainer				
Stretching / Warmup	☐ Rowing Machine				
YES___ NO___	☐ Stair Climber				
Trainer/Instructor:	☐ Stationary Bike				
	☐ Treadmill				
Exercise Buddy:					

Strength Training (Free weights, crunches, machine weights, etc.)

Today's Focus: Upper Body ☐   Lower Body ☐   Abs ☐

Muscle Group	Action or Equipment	SET 1 Reps Wt.	SET 2 Reps Wt.	SET 3 Reps Wt.	SET 4 Reps Wt.	Ease 1-10

COMMENTS: (Problems or injuries, overall mood, best/worst moment, etc.)

Other Exercise (outside the gym)

Activity	Hrs./Min./Qty.	Intensity	Cal. Burn
		Low Med. High	

Dietary Notes	CALORIES	FAT GMS.	CARBS	PROTEIN
Breakfast				
Snack				
Lunch				
Snack				
Dinner				
Snack				
GRAND TOTALS...				

Water (8 oz. glasses)

☐ ☐ ☐ ☐ ☐
☐ ☐ ☐ ☐ ☐

Vitamins, Supplements

NAME / STRENGTH   QTY.

_____
_____
_____
_____
_____
_____
_____
_____

OTHER NOTES:

Met today's goals?

0%   25%   50%   75%   100%

		Week #		
Date		Day #		Day of the Week

Cardio Workout (in the gym)

		Min.	Pace/ setting	Heart rate	Cal. burn
Time of Day: start / finish	☐ Aerobics Class				
	☐ Elliptical Trainer				
Stretching / Warmup	☐ Rowing Machine				
YES___ NO___	☐ Stair Climber				
Trainer/Instructor:	☐ Stationary Bike				
	☐ Treadmill				
Exercise Buddy:					

Strength Training (Free weights, crunches, machine weights, etc.)

Today's Focus: **Upper Body** ☐   **Lower Body** ☐   **Abs** ☐

Muscle Group	Action or Equipment	SET 1 Reps Wt.	SET 2 Reps Wt.	SET 3 Reps Wt.	SET 4 Reps Wt.	Ease 1-10

COMMENTS: (Problems or injuries, overall mood, best/worst moment, etc.)

Other Exercise (outside the gym)

Activity	Hrs./Min./Qty.	Intensity	Cal. Burn
		Low Med. High	

Dietary Notes	CALORIES	FAT GMS	CARBS	PROTEIN
Breakfast				
Snack				
Lunch				
Snack				
Dinner				
Snack				
GRAND TOTALS...				

Water (8 oz. glasses)

☐ ☐ ☐ ☐ ☐
☐ ☐ ☐ ☐ ☐

Vitamins, Supplements

NAME / STRENGTH   QTY.

_____

_____

_____

_____

_____

_____

_____

_____

OTHER NOTES:

Met today's goals?

0%   25%   50%   75%   100%

	Week #	
Date	Day #	Day of the Week

Cardio Workout (in the gym)

	Min.	Pace/ setting	Heart rate	Cal. burn

Time of Day:
start / finish

Stretching / Warmup
YES___   NO___

Trainer/Instructor:

Exercise Buddy:

- ☐ Aerobics Class
- ☐ Elliptical Trainer
- ☐ Rowing Machine
- ☐ Stair Climber
- ☐ Stationary Bike
- ☐ Treadmill

Strength Training (Free weights, crunches, machine weights, etc.)

Today's Focus: Upper Body ☐   **Lower Body** ☐   **Abs** ☐

Muscle Group	Action or Equipment	SET 1 Reps	Wt.	SET 2 Reps	Wt.	SET 3 Reps	Wt.	SET 4 Reps	Wt.	Ease 1-10

COMMENTS: (Problems or injuries, overall mood, best/worst moment, etc.)

Other Exercise (outside the gym)

Activity	Hrs./Min./Qty.	Intensity	Cal. Burn
		Low Med. High	

Dietary Notes	CALORIES	FAT GMS	CARBS	PROTEIN
Breakfast				
Snack				
Lunch				
Snack				
Dinner				
Snack				
GRAND TOTALS...				

Water (8 oz. glasses)

☐ ☐ ☐ ☐ ☐
☐ ☐ ☐ ☐ ☐

Vitamins, Supplements

NAME / STRENGTH   QTY.

OTHER NOTES:

Met today's goals?

0%   25%   50%   75%   100%

Date	Week #	
	Day #	Day of the Week

Cardio Workout (in the gym)

	Min.	Pace/ setting	Heart rate	Cal. burn

Time of Day:	
start / finish	☐ Aerobics Class
	☐ Elliptical Trainer
Stretching / Warmup	☐ Rowing Machine
YES___ NO___	☐ Stair Climber
	☐ Stationary Bike
Trainer/Instructor:	☐ Treadmill
Exercise Buddy:	

Strength Training (Free weights, crunches, machine weights, etc.)

Today's Focus: Upper Body ☐ **Lower Body** ☐ **Abs** ☐

Muscle Group	Action or Equipment	SET 1 Reps Wt.	SET 2 Reps Wt.	SET 3 Reps Wt.	SET 4 Reps Wt.	Ease 1-10

COMMENTS: (Problems or injuries, overall mood, best/worst moment, etc.)

Other Exercise (outside the gym)

Activity	Hrs./Min./Qty.	Intensity	Cal. Burn
		Low Med. High	

Dietary Notes	CALORIES	FAT GMS	CARBS	PROTEIN
Breakfast				
Snack				
Lunch				
Snack				
Dinner				
Snack				
GRAND TOTALS...				

Water (8 oz. glasses)

☐ ☐ ☐ ☐ ☐
☐ ☐ ☐ ☐ ☐

Vitamins, Supplements

NAME / STRENGTH   QTY.

OTHER NOTES:

Met today's goals?

0%   25%   50%   75%   100%

MemoryMinder Journals, Inc. ©

Cardio Workout (in the gym)

		Min.	Pace/ setting	Heart rate	Cal. burn
	☐ Aerobics Class				
Time of Day:	☐ Elliptical Trainer				
start / finish	☐ Rowing Machine				
Stretching / Warmup	☐ Stair Climber				
YES___ NO___	☐ Stationary Bike				
Trainer/Instructor:	☐ Treadmill				
Exercise Buddy:					

Strength Training (Free weights, crunches, machine weights, etc.)

Today's Focus: Upper Body ☐ **Lower Body** ☐ **Abs** ☐

Muscle Group	Action or Equipment	SET 1 Reps	Wt.	SET 2 Reps	Wt.	SET 3 Reps	Wt.	SET 4 Reps	Wt.	Ease 1-10

COMMENTS: (Problems or injuries, overall mood, best/worst moment, etc.)

Other Exercise (outside the gym)

Activity	Hrs./Min./Qty.	Intensity	Cal. Burn
		Low Med. High	

Dietary Notes	CALORIES	FAT GMS	CARBS	PROTEIN
Breakfast				
Snack				
Lunch				
Snack				
Dinner				
Snack				
GRAND TOTALS...				

Water (8 oz. glasses)

☐ ☐ ☐ ☐ ☐
☐ ☐ ☐ ☐ ☐

Vitamins, Supplements

NAME / STRENGTH   QTY.

OTHER NOTES:

Met today's goals?

0%   25%   50%   75%   100%

Date	Week #	
	Day #	Day of the Week

Cardio Workout (in the gym)

	Min.	Pace/ setting	Heart rate	Cal. burn

Time of Day:

start / finish

Stretching / Warmup

YES___ NO___

Trainer/Instructor:

Exercise Buddy:

	Min.	Pace/ setting	Heart rate	Cal. burn
☐ Aerobics Class				
☐ Elliptical Trainer				
☐ Rowing Machine				
☐ Stair Climber				
☐ Stationary Bike				
☐ Treadmill				

Strength Training (Free weights, crunches, machine weights, etc.)

Today's Focus: Upper Body ☐ **Lower Body** ☐ **Abs** ☐

Muscle Group	Action or Equipment	SET 1 Reps Wt.	SET 2 Reps Wt.	SET 3 Reps Wt.	SET 4 Reps Wt.	Ease 1-10

COMMENTS: (Problems or injuries, overall mood, best/worst moment, etc.)

Other Exercise (outside the gym)

Activity	Hrs./Min./Qty.	Intensity	Cal. Burn
		Low Med. High	

Dietary Notes	CALORIES	FAT GMS	CARBS	PROTEIN
Breakfast				
Snack				
Lunch				
Snack				
Dinner				
Snack				
GRAND TOTALS...				

Water (8 oz. glasses)

☐ ☐ ☐ ☐ ☐
☐ ☐ ☐ ☐ ☐

Vitamins, Supplements

NAME / STRENGTH   QTY.

_____
_____
_____
_____
_____
_____
_____
_____

OTHER NOTES:

Met today's goals?

0%   25%   50%   75%   100%

MemoryMinder Journals, Inc.©

Cardio Workout (in the gym)

	Min.	Pace/ setting	Heart rate	Cal. burn
Time of Day:				
start / finish				
☐ Aerobics Class				
☐ Elliptical Trainer				
Stretching / Warmup	☐ Rowing Machine			
YES___ NO___	☐ Stair Climber			
	☐ Stationary Bike			
Trainer/Instructor:	☐ Treadmill			
Exercise Buddy:				

Strength Training (Free weights, crunches, machine weights, etc.)

Today's Focus: Upper Body ☐ **Lower Body** ☐ **Abs** ☐

Muscle Group	Action or Equipment	SET 1 Reps Wt.	SET 2 Reps Wt.	SET 3 Reps Wt.	SET 4 Reps Wt.	Ease 1-10

COMMENTS: (Problems or injuries, overall mood, best/worst moment, etc.)

Other Exercise (outside the gym)

Activity	Hrs./Min./Qty.	Intensity	Cal. Burn
		Low Med. High	

Dietary Notes	CALORIES	FAT GMS	CARBS	PROTEIN
Breakfast				
Snack				
Lunch				
Snack				
Dinner				
Snack				
GRAND TOTALS...				

Water (8 oz. glasses)

☐ ☐ ☐ ☐ ☐
☐ ☐ ☐ ☐ ☐

Vitamins, Supplements

NAME / STRENGTH   QTY.

MemoryMinder Journals, Inc. ©

OTHER NOTES:

Met today's goals?

| 0% | 25% | 50% | 75% | 100% |

Date	Week #	
	Day #	Day of the Week

Cardio Workout (in the gym)

	Min.	Pace/ setting	Heart rate	Cal. burn
☐ Aerobics Class				
☐ Elliptical Trainer				
☐ Rowing Machine				
☐ Stair Climber				
☐ Stationary Bike				
☐ Treadmill				

Time of Day:

start / finish

Stretching / Warmup

YES___ NO___

Trainer/Instructor:

Exercise Buddy:

Strength Training (Free weights, crunches, machine weights, etc.)

Today's Focus: Upper Body ☐ **Lower Body** ☐ **Abs** ☐

Muscle Group	Action or Equipment	SET 1 Reps Wt.	SET 2 Reps Wt.	SET 3 Reps Wt.	SET 4 Reps Wt.	Ease 1-10

COMMENTS: (Problems or injuries, overall mood, best/worst moment, etc.)

Other Exercise (outside the gym)

Activity	Hrs./Min./Qty.	Intensity	Cal. Burn
		Low Med. High	

Dietary Notes	CALORIES	FAT GMS	CARBS	PROTEIN
Breakfast				
Snack				
Lunch				
Snack				
Dinner				
Snack				
GRAND TOTALS...				

Water (8 oz. glasses)

☐ ☐ ☐ ☐ ☐
☐ ☐ ☐ ☐ ☐

Vitamins, Supplements
NAME / STRENGTH   QTY.

_____

_____

_____

_____

_____

_____

_____

OTHER NOTES:

Met today's goals?

0%   25%   50%   75%   100%

MemoryMinder Journals, Inc.©

Cardio Workout (in the gym)

		Min.	Pace/ setting	Heart rate	Cal. burn
Time of Day: start / finish	☐ Aerobics Class				
	☐ Elliptical Trainer				
Stretching / Warmup	☐ Rowing Machine				
YES___ NO___	☐ Stair Climber				
Trainer/Instructor:	☐ Stationary Bike				
	☐ Treadmill				
Exercise Buddy:					

Strength Training (Free weights, crunches, machine weights, etc.)

Today's Focus: Upper Body ☐ **Lower Body** ☐ **Abs** ☐

Muscle Group	Action or Equipment	SET 1 Reps Wt.	SET 2 Reps Wt.	SET 3 Reps Wt.	SET 4 Reps Wt.	Ease 1-10

COMMENTS: (Problems or injuries, overall mood, best/worst moment, etc.)

Other Exercise (outside the gym)

Activity	Hrs./Min./Qty.	Intensity	Cal. Burn
		Low Med. High	

Dietary Notes	CALORIES	FAT GMS	CARBS	PROTEIN	Water (8 oz. glasses)
Breakfast					☐ ☐ ☐ ☐ ☐ ☐ ☐ ☐ ☐ ☐
Snack					
Lunch					
Snack					
Dinner					
Snack					
GRAND TOTALS...					

Vitamins, Supplements

NAME / STRENGTH   QTY.

_____

_____

_____

_____

_____

_____

_____

_____

OTHER NOTES:

Met today's goals?

0%   25%   50%   75%   100%

MemoryMinder Journals, Inc. ©

Date	Week #	
	Day #	Day of the Week

Cardio Workout (in the gym)

	Min.	Pace/ setting	Heart rate	Cal. burn

Time of Day:					

start / finish

☐ Aerobics Class				
☐ Elliptical Trainer				
☐ Rowing Machine				
☐ Stair Climber				
☐ Stationary Bike				
☐ Treadmill				

Stretching / Warmup

YES___ NO___

Trainer/Instructor:

Exercise Buddy:

Strength Training (Free weights, crunches, machine weights, etc.)

Today's Focus: Upper Body ☐   Lower Body ☐   Abs ☐

Muscle Group	Action or Equipment	SET 1 Reps Wt.	SET 2 Reps Wt.	SET 3 Reps Wt.	SET 4 Reps Wt.	Ease 1-10

COMMENTS: (Problems or injuries, overall mood, best/worst moment, etc.)

Other Exercise (outside the gym)

Activity	Hrs./Min./Qty.	Intensity	Cal. Burn
		Low Med. High	

Dietary Notes	CALORIES	FAT GMS	CARBS	PROTEIN
Breakfast				
Snack				
Lunch				
Snack				
Dinner				
Snack				
GRAND TOTALS...				

Water (8 oz. glasses)

☐ ☐ ☐ ☐ ☐
☐ ☐ ☐ ☐ ☐

Vitamins, Supplements

NAME / STRENGTH   QTY.

_____
_____
_____
_____
_____
_____
_____
_____

OTHER NOTES:

Met today's goals?

0%   25%   50%   75%   100%

MemoryMinder Journals, Inc. ©

Date	Week #	
	Day #	Day of the Week

Cardio Workout (in the gym)

	Min.	Pace/ setting	Heart rate	Cal. burn
☐ Aerobics Class				
☐ Elliptical Trainer				
☐ Rowing Machine				
☐ Stair Climber				
☐ Stationary Bike				
☐ Treadmill				

Time of Day:

start / finish

Stretching / Warmup

YES___   NO___

Trainer/Instructor:

Exercise Buddy:

Strength Training (Free weights, crunches, machine weights, etc.)

Today's Focus: Upper Body ☐   **Lower Body** ☐   **Abs** ☐

Muscle Group	Action or Equipment	SET 1 Reps	Wt.	SET 2 Reps	Wt.	SET 3 Reps	Wt.	SET 4 Reps	Wt.	Ease 1-10

COMMENTS: (Problems or injuries, overall mood, best/worst moment, etc.)

Other Exercise (outside the gym)

Activity	Hrs./Min./Qty.	Intensity	Cal. Burn
		Low Med. High	

Dietary Notes	CALORIES	FAT GMS	CARBS	PROTEIN
Breakfast				
Snack				
Lunch				
Snack				
Dinner				
Snack				
GRAND TOTALS...				

Water (8 oz. glasses)

☐ ☐ ☐ ☐ ☐
☐ ☐ ☐ ☐ ☐

Vitamins, Supplements

NAME / STRENGTH   QTY.

_____
_____
_____
_____
_____
_____
_____
_____

OTHER NOTES:

Met today's goals?

0%   25%   50%   75%   100%

MemoryMinder Journals, Inc.©

Date	Week #	
	Day #	Day of the Week

Cardio Workout (in the gym)

		Min.	Pace/ setting	Heart rate	Cal. burn
Time of Day: start / finish	☐ Aerobics Class				
	☐ Elliptical Trainer				
Stretching / Warmup	☐ Rowing Machine				
YES___ NO___	☐ Stair Climber				
Trainer/Instructor:	☐ Stationary Bike				
	☐ Treadmill				
Exercise Buddy:					

Strength Training (Free weights, crunches, machine weights, etc.)

Today's Focus: Upper Body ☐ **Lower Body** ☐ **Abs** ☐

Muscle Group	Action or Equipment	SET 1 Reps Wt.	SET 2 Reps Wt.	SET 3 Reps Wt.	SET 4 Reps Wt.	Ease 1-10

COMMENTS: (Problems or injuries, overall mood, best/worst moment, etc.)

Other Exercise (outside the gym)

Activity	Hrs./Min./Qty.	Intensity	Cal. Burn
		Low · Med. · High	

Dietary Notes

	CALORIES	FAT GMS	CARBS	PROTEIN
Breakfast				
Snack				
Lunch				
Snack				
Dinner				
Snack				
GRAND TOTALS...				

Water (8 oz. glasses)

☐ ☐ ☐ ☐ ☐
☐ ☐ ☐ ☐ ☐

Vitamins, Supplements

NAME / STRENGTH   QTY.

_____ _____
_____ _____
_____ _____
_____ _____
_____ _____
_____ _____
_____ _____

OTHER NOTES:

Met today's goals?

| 0% | 25% | 50% | 75% | 100% |

Cardio Workout (in the gym)

	Min.	Pace/ setting	Heart rate	Cal. burn

Time of Day:	☐ Aerobics Class				
start / finish	☐ Elliptical Trainer				
Stretching / Warmup	☐ Rowing Machine				
YES___ NO___	☐ Stair Climber				
Trainer/Instructor:	☐ Stationary Bike				
	☐ Treadmill				
Exercise Buddy:					

Strength Training (Free weights, crunches, machine weights, etc.)

Today's Focus: Upper Body ☐   **Lower Body** ☐   **Abs** ☐

Muscle Group	Action or Equipment	SET 1 Reps Wt.	SET 2 Reps Wt.	SET 3 Reps Wt.	SET 4 Reps Wt.	Ease 1-10

COMMENTS: (Problems or injuries, overall mood, best/worst moment, etc.)

Other Exercise (outside the gym)

Activity	Hrs./Min./Qty.	Intensity	Cal. Burn
		Low Med. High	

Dietary Notes	CALORIES	FAT GMS	CARBS	PROTEIN
Breakfast				
Snack				
Lunch				
Snack				
Dinner				
Snack				
GRAND TOTALS...				

Water (8 oz. glasses)

☐ ☐ ☐ ☐ ☐
☐ ☐ ☐ ☐ ☐

Vitamins, Supplements

NAME / STRENGTH   QTY.

OTHER NOTES:

Met today's goals?

0%   25%   50%   75%   100%

	Week #	
Date	Day #	Day of the Week

Cardio Workout (in the gym)

		Min.	Pace/ setting	Heart rate	Cal. burn
Time of Day:	☐ Aerobics Class				
start / finish	☐ Elliptical Trainer				
Stretching / Warmup	☐ Rowing Machine				
YES___ NO___	☐ Stair Climber				
	☐ Stationary Bike				
Trainer/Instructor:	☐ Treadmill				
Exercise Buddy:					

Strength Training (Free weights, crunches, machine weights, etc.)

Today's Focus: Upper Body ☐ **Lower Body** ☐ **Abs** ☐

Muscle Group	Action or Equipment	SET 1 Reps Wt.	SET 2 Reps Wt.	SET 3 Reps Wt.	SET 4 Reps Wt.	Ease 1-10

COMMENTS: (Problems or injuries, overall mood, best/worst moment, etc.)

MemoryMinder Journals, Inc.©

Other Exercise (outside the gym)

Activity	Hrs./Min./Qty.	Intensity	Cal. Burn
		Low Med. High	

Dietary Notes

	CALORIES	FAT GMS	CARBS	PROTEIN
Breakfast				
Snack				
Lunch				
Snack				
Dinner				
Snack				
GRAND TOTALS...				

Water (8 oz. glasses)

☐ ☐ ☐ ☐ ☐
☐ ☐ ☐ ☐ ☐

Vitamins, Supplements

NAME / STRENGTH   QTY.

_____

_____

_____

_____

_____

_____

_____

_____

OTHER NOTES:

Met today's goals?

| 0% | 25% | 50% | 75% | 100% |

MemoryMinder Journals, Inc. ©

	Week #	
Date	Day #	Day of the Week

Cardio Workout (in the gym)

		Min.	Pace/ setting	Heart rate	Cal. burn
Time of Day:	☐ Aerobics Class				
start / finish	☐ Elliptical Trainer				
Stretching / Warmup	☐ Rowing Machine				
YES___ NO___	☐ Stair Climber				
Trainer/Instructor:	☐ Stationary Bike				
	☐ Treadmill				
Exercise Buddy:					

Strength Training (Free weights, crunches, machine weights, etc.)

Today's Focus: Upper Body ☐   **Lower Body** ☐   **Abs** ☐

Muscle Group	Action or Equipment	SET 1 Reps Wt.	SET 2 Reps Wt.	SET 3 Reps Wt.	SET 4 Reps Wt.	Ease 1-10

COMMENTS: (Problems or injuries, overall mood, best/worst moment, etc.)

Other Exercise (outside the gym)

Activity	Hrs./Min./Qty.	Intensity	Cal. Burn
		Low Med. High	

Dietary Notes	CALORIES	FAT GMS	CARBS	PROTEIN
Breakfast				
Snack				
Lunch				
Snack				
Dinner				
Snack				
GRAND TOTALS...				

Water (8 oz. glasses)

☐ ☐ ☐ ☐ ☐
☐ ☐ ☐ ☐ ☐

Vitamins, Supplements

NAME / STRENGTH	QTY.

OTHER NOTES:

Met today's goals?

0%   25%   50%   75%   100%

MemoryMinder Journals, Inc. ©

	Week #	
Date	Day #	Day of the Week

Cardio Workout (in the gym)

		Min.	Pace/ setting	Heart rate	Cal. burn

Time of Day:	☐ Aerobics Class				
start / finish	☐ Elliptical Trainer				
Stretching / Warmup	☐ Rowing Machine				
YES___ NO___	☐ Stair Climber				
Trainer/Instructor:	☐ Stationary Bike				
	☐ Treadmill				
Exercise Buddy:					

Strength Training (Free weights, crunches, machine weights, etc.)

Today's Focus: Upper Body ☐	Lower Body ☐	Abs ☐

Muscle Group	Action or Equipment	SET 1 Reps Wt.	SET 2 Reps Wt.	SET 3 Reps Wt.	SET 4 Reps Wt.	Ease 1-10

COMMENTS: (Problems or injuries, overall mood, best/worst moment, etc.)

Other Exercise (outside the gym)

Activity	Hrs./Min./Qty.	Intensity	Cal. Burn
		Low Med. High	

Dietary Notes	CALORIES	FAT GMS	CARBS	PROTEIN
Breakfast				
Snack				
Lunch				
Snack				
Dinner				
Snack				
GRAND TOTALS...				

Water (8 oz. glasses)

☐ ☐ ☐ ☐ ☐
☐ ☐ ☐ ☐ ☐

Vitamins, Supplements

NAME / STRENGTH   QTY.

_____

_____

_____

_____

_____

_____

_____

_____

OTHER NOTES:

Met today's goals?

| 0% | 25% | 50% | 75% | 100% |

MemoryMinder Journals, Inc.©

		Week #		
	Date	Day #		Day of the Week

Cardio Workout (in the gym)

		Min.	Pace/ setting	Heart rate	Cal. burn
Time of Day: start / finish	☐ Aerobics Class				
	☐ Elliptical Trainer				
Stretching / Warmup YES___ NO___	☐ Rowing Machine				
	☐ Stair Climber				
Trainer/Instructor:	☐ Stationary Bike				
	☐ Treadmill				
Exercise Buddy:					

Strength Training (Free weights, crunches, machine weights, etc.)

Today's Focus: Upper Body ☐   **Lower Body** ☐   **Abs** ☐

Muscle Group	Action or Equipment	SET 1 Reps	Wt.	SET 2 Reps	Wt.	SET 3 Reps	Wt.	SET 4 Reps	Wt.	Ease 1-10

COMMENTS: (Problems or injuries, overall mood, best/worst moment, etc.)

Other Exercise (outside the gym)

Activity	Hrs./Min./Qty.	Intensity	Cal. Burn
		Low Med. High	

Dietary Notes	CALORIES	FAT GMS	CARBS	PROTEIN
Breakfast				
Snack				
Lunch				
Snack				
Dinner				
Snack				
GRAND TOTALS...				

Water (8 oz. glasses)

☐ ☐ ☐ ☐ ☐
☐ ☐ ☐ ☐ ☐

Vitamins, Supplements

NAME / STRENGTH   QTY.

OTHER NOTES:

Met today's goals?

0%   25%   50%   75%   100%

MemoryMinder Journals, Inc.©

Date	Week #	
	Day #	Day of the Week

Cardio Workout (in the gym)

	Min.	Pace/ setting	Heart rate	Cal. burn
☐ Aerobics Class				
☐ Elliptical Trainer				
☐ Rowing Machine				
☐ Stair Climber				
☐ Stationary Bike				
☐ Treadmill				

Time of Day:

start / finish

Stretching / Warmup

YES___ NO___

Trainer/Instructor:

Exercise Buddy:

Strength Training (Free weights, crunches, machine weights, etc.)

Today's Focus: Upper Body ☐   Lower Body ☐   Abs ☐

Muscle Group	Action or Equipment	SET 1 Reps Wt.	SET 2 Reps Wt.	SET 3 Reps Wt.	SET 4 Reps Wt.	Ease 1-10

COMMENTS: (Problems or injuries, overall mood, best/worst moment, etc.)

Other Exercise (outside the gym)

Activity	Hrs./Min./Qty.	Intensity	Cal. Burn
		Low Med. High	

Dietary Notes	CALORIES	FAT GMS	CARBS	PROTEIN
Breakfast				
Snack				
Lunch				
Snack				
Dinner				
Snack				
GRAND TOTALS...				

Water (8 oz. glasses)

☐ ☐ ☐ ☐ ☐
☐ ☐ ☐ ☐ ☐

Vitamins, Supplements

NAME / STRENGTH   QTY.

_____

_____

_____

_____

_____

_____

_____

_____

OTHER NOTES:

Met today's goals?

| 0% | 25% | 50% | 75% | 100% |

MemoryMinder Journals, Inc. ©

	Week #	
_____ Date	Day #	_____ Day of the Week

Cardio Workout (in the gym)

	Min.	Pace/ setting	Heart rate	Cal. burn
☐ Aerobics Class				
☐ Elliptical Trainer				
☐ Rowing Machine				
☐ Stair Climber				
☐ Stationary Bike				
☐ Treadmill				

Time of Day:

start / finish

Stretching / Warmup

YES___   NO___

Trainer/Instructor:

Exercise Buddy:

Strength Training (Free weights, crunches, machine weights, etc.)

Today's Focus: Upper Body ☐   Lower Body ☐   Abs ☐

Muscle Group	Action or Equipment	SET 1 Reps Wt.	SET 2 Reps Wt.	SET 3 Reps Wt.	SET 4 Reps Wt.	Ease 1-10

COMMENTS: (Problems or injuries, overall mood, best/worst moment, etc.)

Other Exercise (outside the gym)

Activity	Hrs./Min./Qty.	Intensity	Cal. Burn
		Low Med. High	

Dietary Notes	CALORIES	FAT GMS	CARBS	PROTEIN
Breakfast				
Snack				
Lunch				
Snack				
Dinner				
Snack				
GRAND TOTALS...				

Water (8 oz. glasses)

☐ ☐ ☐ ☐ ☐
☐ ☐ ☐ ☐ ☐

Vitamins, Supplements

NAME / STRENGTH   QTY.

_____
_____
_____
_____
_____
_____
_____
_____

OTHER NOTES:

Met today's goals?

| 0% | 25% | 50% | 75% | 100% |

MemoryMinder Journals, Inc.©

Date	Week #	
	Day #	Day of the Week

Cardio Workout (in the gym)

	Min.	Pace/ setting	Heart rate	Cal. burn
☐ Aerobics Class				
☐ Elliptical Trainer				
☐ Rowing Machine				
☐ Stair Climber				
☐ Stationary Bike				
☐ Treadmill				

Time of Day:

start / finish

Stretching / Warmup

YES___   NO___

Trainer/Instructor:

Exercise Buddy:

Strength Training (Free weights, crunches, machine weights, etc.)

Today's Focus: Upper Body ☐   Lower Body ☐   Abs ☐

Muscle Group	Action or Equipment	SET 1 Reps Wt.	SET 2 Reps Wt.	SET 3 Reps Wt.	SET 4 Reps Wt.	Ease 1-10

COMMENTS: (Problems or injuries, overall mood, best/worst moment, etc.)

Other Exercise (outside the gym)

Activity	Hrs./Min./Qty.	Intensity	Cal. Burn
		Low Med. High	

Dietary Notes	CALORIES	FAT GMS.	CARBS	PROTEIN
Breakfast				
Snack				
Lunch				
Snack				
Dinner				
Snack				
GRAND TOTALS...				

Water (8 oz. glasses)

☐ ☐ ☐ ☐ ☐
☐ ☐ ☐ ☐ ☐

Vitamins, Supplements

NAME / STRENGTH   QTY.

_____
_____
_____
_____
_____
_____
_____
_____

OTHER NOTES:

Met today's goals?

| 0% | 25% | 50% | 75% | 100% |

MemoryMinder Journals, Inc. ©

Date	Week #	
	Day #	Day of the Week

Cardio Workout (in the gym)

	Min.	Pace/ setting	Heart rate	Cal. burn

Time of Day:

start / finish

☐ Aerobics Class	
☐ Elliptical Trainer	
☐ Rowing Machine	
☐ Stair Climber	
☐ Stationary Bike	
☐ Treadmill	

Stretching / Warmup

YES___ NO___

Trainer/Instructor:

Exercise Buddy:

Strength Training (Free weights, crunches, machine weights, etc.)

Today's Focus: Upper Body ☐ **Lower Body** ☐ **Abs** ☐

Muscle Group	Action or Equipment	SET 1 Reps Wt.	SET 2 Reps Wt.	SET 3 Reps Wt.	SET 4 Reps Wt.	Ease 1-10

COMMENTS: (Problems or injuries, overall mood, best/worst moment, etc.)

MemoryMinder Journals, Inc. ©

Other Exercise (outside the gym)

Activity	Hrs./Min./Qty.	Intensity	Cal. Burn
		Low Med. High	

Dietary Notes	CALORIES	FAT GMS	CARBS	PROTEIN
Breakfast				
Snack				
Lunch				
Snack				
Dinner				
Snack				
GRAND TOTALS...				

Water (8 oz. glasses)

☐ ☐ ☐ ☐ ☐
☐ ☐ ☐ ☐ ☐

Vitamins, Supplements

NAME / STRENGTH   QTY.

_____
_____
_____
_____
_____
_____
_____

OTHER NOTES:

Met today's goals?

0%   25%   50%   75%   100%

Date	Week #	
	Day #	Day of the Week

Cardio Workout (in the gym)

	Min.	Pace/ setting	Heart rate	Cal. burn
☐ Aerobics Class				
☐ Elliptical Trainer				
☐ Rowing Machine				
☐ Stair Climber				
☐ Stationary Bike				
☐ Treadmill				

Time of Day:

start / finish

Stretching / Warmup

YES___   NO___

Trainer/Instructor:

Exercise Buddy:

Strength Training (Free weights, crunches, machine weights, etc.)

Today's Focus: Upper Body ☐   **Lower Body** ☐   **Abs** ☐

Muscle Group	Action or Equipment	SET 1 Reps Wt.	SET 2 Reps Wt.	SET 3 Reps Wt.	SET 4 Reps Wt.	Ease 1-10

COMMENTS: (Problems or injuries, overall mood, best/worst moment, etc.)

Other Exercise (outside the gym)

Activity	Hrs./Min./Qty.	Intensity	Cal. Burn
		Low Med. High	

Dietary Notes	CALORIES	FAT GMS	CARBS	PROTEIN
Breakfast				
Snack				
Lunch				
Snack				
Dinner				
Snack				
GRAND TOTALS...				

Water (8 oz. glasses)

☐ ☐ ☐ ☐ ☐
☐ ☐ ☐ ☐ ☐

Vitamins, Supplements

NAME / STRENGTH   QTY.

_____

_____

_____

_____

_____

_____

_____

_____

OTHER NOTES:

Met today's goals?

| 0% | 25% | 50% | 75% | 100% |

MemoryMinder Journals, Inc. ©

Date	Week #	
	Day #	Day of the Week

Cardio Workout (in the gym)

		Min.	Pace/ setting	Heart rate	Cal. burn
Time of Day:	☐ Aerobics Class				
start / finish	☐ Elliptical Trainer				
Stretching / Warmup	☐ Rowing Machine				
YES___ NO___	☐ Stair Climber				
Trainer/Instructor:	☐ Stationary Bike				
	☐ Treadmill				
Exercise Buddy:					

Strength Training (Free weights, crunches, machine weights, etc.)

Today's Focus: Upper Body ☐   Lower Body ☐   Abs ☐

Muscle Group	Action or Equipment	SET 1 Reps Wt.	SET 2 Reps Wt.	SET 3 Reps Wt.	SET 4 Reps Wt.	Ease 1-10

COMMENTS: (Problems or injuries, overall mood, best/worst moment, etc.)

Other Exercise (outside the gym)

Activity	Hrs./Min./Qty.	Intensity	Cal. Burn
		Low Med. High	

Dietary Notes

	CALORIES	FAT GMS	CARBS	PROTEIN
Breakfast				
Snack				
Lunch				
Snack				
Dinner				
Snack				
GRAND TOTALS...				

Water (8 oz. glasses)

☐ ☐ ☐ ☐ ☐
☐ ☐ ☐ ☐ ☐

Vitamins, Supplements

NAME / STRENGTH   QTY.

_____

_____

_____

_____

_____

_____

_____

OTHER NOTES:

Met today's goals?

0%   25%   50%   75%   100%

Date	Week # Day #	Day of the Week

Cardio Workout (in the gym)

		Min.	Pace/ setting	Heart rate	Cal. burn
Time of Day: start / finish	☐ Aerobics Class				
	☐ Elliptical Trainer				
Stretching / Warmup YES___ NO___	☐ Rowing Machine				
	☐ Stair Climber				
Trainer/Instructor:	☐ Stationary Bike				
	☐ Treadmill				
Exercise Buddy:					

Strength Training (Free weights, crunches, machine weights, etc.)

Today's Focus: Upper Body ☐ **Lower Body** ☐ **Abs** ☐

Muscle Group	Action or Equipment	SET 1 Reps Wt.	SET 2 Reps Wt.	SET 3 Reps Wt.	SET 4 Reps Wt.	Ease 1-10

COMMENTS: (Problems or injuries, overall mood, best/worst moment, etc.)

Other Exercise (outside the gym)

Activity	Hrs./Min./Qty.	Intensity	Cal. Burn
		Low Med. High	

Dietary Notes	CALORIES	FAT GMS	CARBS	PROTEIN
Breakfast				
Snack				
Lunch				
Snack				
Dinner				
Snack				
GRAND TOTALS...				

Water (8 oz. glasses)

☐ ☐ ☐ ☐ ☐
☐ ☐ ☐ ☐ ☐

Vitamins, Supplements

NAME / STRENGTH   QTY.

OTHER NOTES:

Met today's goals?

0%   25%   50%   75%   100%

MemoryMinder Journals, Inc. ©

	Week #	
Date	Day #	Day of the Week

Cardio Workout (in the gym)

		Min.	Pace/ setting	Heart rate	Cal. burn
Time of Day:	☐ Aerobics Class				
start / finish	☐ Elliptical Trainer				
Stretching / Warmup	☐ Rowing Machine				
YES___ NO___	☐ Stair Climber				
Trainer/Instructor:	☐ Stationary Bike				
	☐ Treadmill				
Exercise Buddy:					

Strength Training (Free weights, crunches, machine weights, etc.)

Today's Focus: **Upper Body** ☐   **Lower Body** ☐   **Abs** ☐

Muscle Group	Action or Equipment	SET 1 Reps Wt.	SET 2 Reps Wt.	SET 3 Reps Wt.	SET 4 Reps Wt.	Ease 1-10

COMMENTS: (Problems or injuries, overall mood, best/worst moment, etc.)

Other Exercise (outside the gym)

Activity	Hrs./Min./Qty.	Intensity Low Med. High	Cal. Burn

Dietary Notes	CALORIES	FAT GMS	CARBS	PROTEIN
Breakfast				
Snack				
Lunch				
Snack				
Dinner				
Snack				
GRAND TOTALS...				

Water (8 oz. glasses)

☐ ☐ ☐ ☐ ☐
☐ ☐ ☐ ☐ ☐

Vitamins, Supplements

NAME / STRENGTH	QTY.

OTHER NOTES:

Met today's goals?

0% 25% 50% 75% 100%

MemoryMinder Journals, Inc.©

Date	Week #	
	Day #	Day of the Week

Cardio Workout (in the gym)

	Min.	Pace/ setting	Heart rate	Cal. burn

Time of Day:

start / finish

Stretching / Warmup

YES___   NO___

Trainer/Instructor:

Exercise Buddy:

Exercise	Min.	Pace/ setting	Heart rate	Cal. burn
☐ Aerobics Class				
☐ Elliptical Trainer				
☐ Rowing Machine				
☐ Stair Climber				
☐ Stationary Bike				
☐ Treadmill				

Strength Training (Free weights, crunches, machine weights, etc.)

Today's Focus: Upper Body ☐ **Lower Body** ☐ **Abs** ☐

Muscle Group	Action or Equipment	SET 1 Reps	Wt.	SET 2 Reps	Wt.	SET 3 Reps	Wt.	SET 4 Reps	Wt.	Ease 1-10

COMMENTS: (Problems or injuries, overall mood, best/worst moment, etc.)

Other Exercise (outside the gym)

Activity	Hrs./Min./Qty.	Intensity	Cal. Burn
		Low Med. High	

Dietary Notes	CALORIES	FAT GMS.	CARBS	PROTEIN
Breakfast				
Snack				
Lunch				
Snack				
Dinner				
Snack				
GRAND TOTALS...				

Water (8 oz. glasses)

☐ ☐ ☐ ☐ ☐
☐ ☐ ☐ ☐ ☐

Vitamins, Supplements

NAME / STRENGTH   QTY.

_____

_____

_____

_____

_____

_____

_____

_____

OTHER NOTES:

MemoryMinder Journals, Inc.©

Met today's goals?

| 0% | 25% | 50% | 75% | 100% |

Cardio Workout (in the gym)

	Min.	Pace/ setting	Heart rate	Cal. burn

Time of Day: start / finish	☐ Aerobics Class				
	☐ Elliptical Trainer				
Stretching / Warmup YES___ NO___	☐ Rowing Machine				
	☐ Stair Climber				
Trainer/Instructor:	☐ Stationary Bike				
	☐ Treadmill				
Exercise Buddy:					

Strength Training (Free weights, crunches, machine weights, etc.)

Today's Focus: Upper Body ☐ Lower Body ☐ Abs ☐

Muscle Group	Action or Equipment	SET 1 Reps	Wt.	SET 2 Reps	Wt.	SET 3 Reps	Wt.	SET 4 Reps	Wt.	Ease 1-10

COMMENTS: (Problems or injuries, overall mood, best/worst moment, etc.)

Other Exercise (outside the gym)

Activity	Hrs./Min./Qty.	Intensity	Cal. Burn
		Low Med. High	

Dietary Notes	CALORIES	FAT GMS	CARBS	PROTEIN
Breakfast				
Snack				
Lunch				
Snack				
Dinner				
Snack				
GRAND TOTALS...				

Water (8 oz. glasses)

☐ ☐ ☐ ☐ ☐
☐ ☐ ☐ ☐ ☐

Vitamins, Supplements

NAME / STRENGTH   QTY.

_____

_____

_____

_____

_____

_____

_____

_____

OTHER NOTES:

Met today's goals?

0%   25%   50%   75%   100%

	Week #	
Date	Day #	Day of the Week

Cardio Workout (in the gym)

		Min.	Pace/ setting	Heart rate	Cal. burn
Time of Day: start / finish	☐ Aerobics Class				
	☐ Elliptical Trainer				
Stretching / Warmup	☐ Rowing Machine				
YES___ NO___	☐ Stair Climber				
Trainer/Instructor:	☐ Stationary Bike				
	☐ Treadmill				
Exercise Buddy:					

Strength Training (Free weights, crunches, machine weights, etc.)

Today's Focus: Upper Body ☐   Lower Body ☐   Abs ☐

Muscle Group	Action or Equipment	SET 1 Reps Wt.	SET 2 Reps Wt.	SET 3 Reps Wt.	SET 4 Reps Wt.	Ease 1-10

COMMENTS: (Problems or injuries, overall mood, best/worst moment, etc.)

Other Exercise (outside the gym)

Activity	Hrs./Min./Qty.	Intensity	Cal. Burn
		Low Med. High	

Dietary Notes	CALORIES	FAT GMS	CARBS	PROTEIN
Breakfast				
Snack				
Lunch				
Snack				
Dinner				
Snack				
GRAND TOTALS...				

Water (8 oz. glasses)

☐ ☐ ☐ ☐ ☐
☐ ☐ ☐ ☐ ☐

Vitamins, Supplements

NAME / STRENGTH   QTY.

OTHER NOTES:

Met today's goals?

0%   25%   50%   75%   100%

Date	Week # Day #	Day of the Week

Cardio Workout (in the gym)

		Min.	Pace/ setting	Heart rate	Cal. burn

Time of Day: start / finish

Stretching / Warmup YES___   NO___

Trainer/Instructor:

Exercise Buddy:

	Min.	Pace/ setting	Heart rate	Cal. burn
☐ Aerobics Class				
☐ Elliptical Trainer				
☐ Rowing Machine				
☐ Stair Climber				
☐ Stationary Bike				
☐ Treadmill				

Strength Training (Free weights, crunches, machine weights, etc.)

Today's Focus: Upper Body ☐   **Lower Body** ☐   **Abs** ☐

Muscle Group	Action or Equipment	SET 1 Reps	Wt.	SET 2 Reps	Wt.	SET 3 Reps	Wt.	SET 4 Reps	Wt.	Ease 1-10

COMMENTS: (Problems or injuries, overall mood, best/worst moment, etc.)

MemoryMinder Journals, Inc. ©

Other Exercise (outside the gym)

Activity	Hrs./Min./Qty.	Intensity	Cal. Burn
		Low Med. High	

Dietary Notes	CALORIES	FAT GMS	CARBS	PROTEIN
Breakfast				
Snack				
Lunch				
Snack				
Dinner				
Snack				
GRAND TOTALS...				

Water (8 oz. glasses)

☐ ☐ ☐ ☐ ☐
☐ ☐ ☐ ☐ ☐

Vitamins, Supplements

NAME / STRENGTH   QTY.

_____

_____

_____

_____

_____

_____

_____

_____

OTHER NOTES:

Met today's goals?

0%   25%   50%   75%   100%

	Week #	
Date	Day #	Day of the Week

Cardio Workout (in the gym)

		Min.	Pace/ setting	Heart rate	Cal. burn
Time of Day: start / finish	☐ Aerobics Class				
	☐ Elliptical Trainer				
Stretching / Warmup	☐ Rowing Machine				
YES___ NO___	☐ Stair Climber				
Trainer/Instructor:	☐ Stationary Bike				
	☐ Treadmill				
Exercise Buddy:					

Strength Training (Free weights, crunches, machine weights, etc.)

Today's Focus: **Upper Body** ☐   **Lower Body** ☐   **Abs** ☐

Muscle Group	Action or Equipment	SET 1 Reps Wt.	SET 2 Reps Wt.	SET 3 Reps Wt.	SET 4 Reps Wt.	Ease 1-10

COMMENTS: (Problems or injuries, overall mood, best/worst moment, etc.)

Other Exercise (outside the gym)

Activity	Hrs./Min./Qty.	Intensity	Cal. Burn
		Low Med. High	

Dietary Notes	CALORIES	FAT GMS.	CARBS	PROTEIN
Breakfast				
Snack				
Lunch				
Snack				
Dinner				
Snack				
GRAND TOTALS...				

Water (8 oz. glasses)

☐ ☐ ☐ ☐ ☐
☐ ☐ ☐ ☐ ☐

Vitamins, Supplements

NAME / STRENGTH   QTY.

OTHER NOTES:

Met today's goals?

| 0% | 25% | 50% | 75% | 100% |

Date	Week # Day #	Day of the Week

Cardio Workout (in the gym)

		Min.	Pace/ setting	Heart rate	Cal. burn
Time of Day: start / finish	☐ Aerobics Class				
	☐ Elliptical Trainer				
Stretching / Warmup YES___ NO___	☐ Rowing Machine				
	☐ Stair Climber				
Trainer/Instructor:	☐ Stationary Bike				
	☐ Treadmill				
Exercise Buddy:					

Strength Training (Free weights, crunches, machine weights, etc.)

Today's Focus: Upper Body ☐ **Lower Body** ☐ **Abs** ☐

Muscle Group	Action or Equipment	SET 1 Reps Wt.	SET 2 Reps Wt.	SET 3 Reps Wt.	SET 4 Reps Wt.	Ease 1-10

COMMENTS: (Problems or injuries, overall mood, best/worst moment, etc.)

Other Exercise (outside the gym)

Activity	Hrs./Min./Qty.	Intensity	Cal. Burn
		Low Med. High	

Dietary Notes	CALORIES	FAT GMS	CARBS	PROTEIN
Breakfast				
Snack				
Lunch				
Snack				
Dinner				
Snack				
GRAND TOTALS...				

Water (8 oz. glasses)

☐ ☐ ☐ ☐ ☐
☐ ☐ ☐ ☐ ☐

Vitamins, Supplements

NAME / STRENGTH   QTY.

OTHER NOTES:

Met today's goals?

0%   25%   50%   75%   100%

	Week #	
Date	Day #	Day of the Week

Cardio Workout (in the gym)

		Min.	Pace/ setting	Heart rate	Cal. burn
Time of Day: __/__ start / finish	☐ Aerobics Class				
	☐ Elliptical Trainer				
Stretching / Warmup	☐ Rowing Machine				
YES___ NO___	☐ Stair Climber				
	☐ Stationary Bike				
Trainer/Instructor:	☐ Treadmill				
Exercise Buddy:					

Strength Training (Free weights, crunches, machine weights, etc.)

Today's Focus: **Upper Body** ☐ **Lower Body** ☐ **Abs** ☐

Muscle Group	Action or Equipment	SET 1 Reps Wt.	SET 2 Reps Wt.	SET 3 Reps Wt.	SET 4 Reps Wt.	Ease 1-10

COMMENTS: (Problems or injuries, overall mood, best/worst moment, etc.)

Other Exercise (outside the gym)

Activity	Hrs./Min./Qty.	Intensity	Cal. Burn
		Low Med. High	

Dietary Notes	CALORIES	FAT GMS	CARBS	PROTEIN
Breakfast				
Snack				
Lunch				
Snack				
Dinner				
Snack				
GRAND TOTALS...				

Water (8 oz. glasses)

☐ ☐ ☐ ☐ ☐
☐ ☐ ☐ ☐ ☐

Vitamins, Supplements

NAME / STRENGTH   QTY.

_____

_____

_____

_____

_____

_____

_____

OTHER NOTES:

Met today's goals?

0%   25%   50%   75%   100%

Date	Week #	
	Day #	Day of the Week

Cardio Workout (in the gym)

	Min.	Pace/ setting	Heart rate	Cal. burn
☐ Aerobics Class				
☐ Elliptical Trainer				
☐ Rowing Machine				
☐ Stair Climber				
☐ Stationary Bike				
☐ Treadmill				

Time of Day:

start / finish

Stretching / Warmup

YES___   NO___

Trainer/Instructor:

Exercise Buddy:

Strength Training (Free weights, crunches, machine weights, etc.)

Today's Focus: Upper Body ☐ **Lower Body** ☐ **Abs** ☐

Muscle Group	Action or Equipment	SET 1 Reps Wt.	SET 2 Reps Wt.	SET 3 Reps Wt.	SET 4 Reps Wt.	Ease 1-10

COMMENTS: (Problems or injuries, overall mood, best/worst moment, etc.)

Other Exercise (outside the gym)

Activity	Hrs./Min./Qty.	Intensity	Cal. Burn
		Low Med. High	

Dietary Notes	CALORIES	FAT GMS	CARBS	PROTEIN
Breakfast				
Snack				
Lunch				
Snack				
Dinner				
Snack				
GRAND TOTALS...				

Water (8 oz. glasses)

☐ ☐ ☐ ☐ ☐
☐ ☐ ☐ ☐ ☐

Vitamins, Supplements

NAME / STRENGTH   QTY.

OTHER NOTES:

Met today's goals?

| 0% | 25% | 50% | 75% | 100% |

MemoryMinder Journals, Inc.©

Cardio Workout (in the gym)

	<u>Min.</u>	Pace/ <u>setting</u>	Heart <u>rate</u>	Cal. <u>burn</u>

Time of Day:

start / finish

Stretching / Warmup

YES___ NO___

Trainer/Instructor:

Exercise Buddy:

☐ Aerobics Class
☐ Elliptical Trainer
☐ Rowing Machine
☐ Stair Climber
☐ Stationary Bike
☐ Treadmill

Strength Training (Free weights, crunches, machine weights, etc.)

Today's Focus: Upper Body ☐ **Lower Body** ☐ **Abs** ☐

Muscle <u>Group</u>	<u>Action or Equipment</u>	SET 1 <u>Reps</u> <u>Wt.</u>	SET 2 <u>Reps</u> <u>Wt.</u>	SET 3 <u>Reps</u> <u>Wt.</u>	SET 4 <u>Reps</u> <u>Wt.</u>	Ease <u>1-10</u>

COMMENTS: (Problems or injuries, overall mood, best/worst moment, etc.)

Other Exercise (outside the gym)

Activity	Hrs./Min./Qty.	Intensity	Cal. Burn
		Low Med. High	

Dietary Notes	CALORIES	FAT GMS	CARBS	PROTEIN
Breakfast				
Snack				
Lunch				
Snack				
Dinner				
Snack				
GRAND TOTALS...				

Water (8 oz. glasses)

☐ ☐ ☐ ☐ ☐
☐ ☐ ☐ ☐

Vitamins, Supplements

NAME / STRENGTH   QTY.

OTHER NOTES:

Met today's goals?

0%   25%   50%   75%   100%

Date	Week #	
	Day #	Day of the Week

Cardio Workout (in the gym)

	Min.	Pace/ setting	Heart rate	Cal. burn

Time of Day:

start / finish

Stretching / Warmup

YES___ NO___

Trainer/Instructor:

Exercise Buddy:

	Min.	Pace/ setting	Heart rate	Cal. burn
☐ Aerobics Class				
☐ Elliptical Trainer				
☐ Rowing Machine				
☐ Stair Climber				
☐ Stationary Bike				
☐ Treadmill				

Strength Training (Free weights, crunches, machine weights, etc.)

Today's Focus: Upper Body ☐   **Lower Body** ☐   **Abs** ☐

Muscle Group	Action or Equipment	SET 1 Reps Wt.	SET 2 Reps Wt.	SET 3 Reps Wt.	SET 4 Reps Wt.	Ease 1-10

COMMENTS: (Problems or injuries, overall mood, best/worst moment, etc.)

Other Exercise (outside the gym)

Activity	Hrs./Min./Qty.	Intensity	Cal. Burn
		Low Med. High	

Dietary Notes	CALORIES	FAT GMS	CARBS	PROTEIN
Breakfast				
Snack				
Lunch				
Snack				
Dinner				
Snack				
GRAND TOTALS...				

Water (8 oz. glasses)

☐ ☐ ☐ ☐ ☐

☐ ☐ ☐ ☐ ☐

Vitamins, Supplements

NAME / STRENGTH   QTY.

OTHER NOTES:

Met today's goals?

0%   25%   50%   75%   100%

MemoryMinder Journals, Inc.©

	Week #		
Date	Day #	Day of the Week	

Cardio Workout (in the gym)

		Min.	Pace/ setting	Heart rate	Cal. burn
Time of Day:	☐ Aerobics Class				
start / finish	☐ Elliptical Trainer				
	☐ Rowing Machine				
Stretching / Warmup	☐ Stair Climber				
YES___ NO___	☐ Stationary Bike				
Trainer/Instructor:	☐ Treadmill				
Exercise Buddy:					

Strength Training (Free weights, crunches, machine weights, etc.)

Today's Focus: Upper Body ☐　**Lower Body** ☐　**Abs** ☐

Muscle Group	Action or Equipment	SET 1 Reps Wt.	SET 2 Reps Wt.	SET 3 Reps Wt.	SET 4 Reps Wt.	Ease 1-10

COMMENTS: (Problems or injuries, overall mood, best/worst moment, etc.)

Other Exercise (outside the gym)

Activity	Hrs./Min./Qty.	Intensity	Cal. Burn
		Low Med. High	

Dietary Notes	CALORIES	FAT GMS	CARBS	PROTEIN
Breakfast				
Snack				
Lunch				
Snack				
Dinner				
Snack				
GRAND TOTALS...				

Water (8 oz. glasses)

☐ ☐ ☐ ☐ ☐
☐ ☐ ☐ ☐ ☐

Vitamins, Supplements
NAME / STRENGTH   QTY.

_____
_____
_____
_____
_____
_____
_____
_____

OTHER NOTES:

Met today's goals?

0%   25%   50%   75%   100%

	Week #	
Date	Day #	Day of the Week

Cardio Workout (in the gym)

		Min.	Pace/ setting	Heart rate	Cal. burn
Time of Day: start / finish	☐ Aerobics Class				
	☐ Elliptical Trainer				
Stretching / Warmup	☐ Rowing Machine				
YES___ NO___	☐ Stair Climber				
Trainer/Instructor:	☐ Stationary Bike				
	☐ Treadmill				
Exercise Buddy:					

Strength Training (Free weights, crunches, machine weights, etc.)

Today's Focus: Upper Body ☐ **Lower Body** ☐ **Abs** ☐

Muscle Group	Action or Equipment	SET 1 Reps Wt.	SET 2 Reps Wt.	SET 3 Reps Wt.	SET 4 Reps Wt.	Ease 1-10

COMMENTS: (Problems or injuries, overall mood, best/worst moment, etc.)

Other Exercise (outside the gym)

Activity	Hrs./Min./Qty.	Intensity	Cal. Burn
		Low Med. High	

Dietary Notes	CALORIES	FAT GMS	CARBS	PROTEIN
Breakfast				
Snack				
Lunch				
Snack				
Dinner				
Snack				
GRAND TOTALS...				

Water (8 oz. glasses)

☐ ☐ ☐ ☐ ☐
☐ ☐ ☐ ☐ ☐

Vitamins, Supplements
NAME / STRENGTH   QTY.

_____
_____
_____
_____
_____
_____
_____
_____

OTHER NOTES:

Met today's goals?

| 0% | 25% | 50% | 75% | 100% |

Cardio Workout (in the gym)

	Min.	Pace/ setting	Heart rate	Cal. burn

Time of Day:

start / finish

☐ Aerobics Class				
☐ Elliptical Trainer				
☐ Rowing Machine				
☐ Stair Climber				
☐ Stationary Bike				
☐ Treadmill				

Stretching / Warmup

YES___ NO___

Trainer/Instructor:

Exercise Buddy:

Strength Training (Free weights, crunches, machine weights, etc.)

Today's Focus: Upper Body ☐   Lower Body ☐   Abs ☐

Muscle Group	Action or Equipment	SET 1 Reps Wt.	SET 2 Reps Wt.	SET 3 Reps Wt.	SET 4 Reps Wt.	Ease 1-10

COMMENTS: (Problems or injuries, overall mood, best/worst moment, etc.)

Other Exercise (outside the gym)

Activity	Hrs./Min./Qty.	Intensity	Cal. Burn
		Low Med. High	

Dietary Notes	CALORIES	FAT GMS.	CARBS	PROTEIN
Breakfast				
Snack				
Lunch				
Snack				
Dinner				
Snack				
GRAND TOTALS...				

Water (8 oz. glasses)

☐ ☐ ☐ ☐ ☐
☐ ☐ ☐ ☐ ☐

Vitamins, Supplements

NAME / STRENGTH   QTY.

OTHER NOTES:

Met today's goals?

0%   25%   50%   75%   100%

MemoryMinder Journals, Inc.©

Cardio Workout (in the gym)

		Min.	Pace/ setting	Heart rate	Cal. burn
Time of Day:	☐ Aerobics Class				
	☐ Elliptical Trainer				
start / finish	☐ Rowing Machine				
Stretching / Warmup	☐ Stair Climber				
YES___ NO___	☐ Stationary Bike				
Trainer/Instructor:	☐ Treadmill				
Exercise Buddy:					

Strength Training (Free weights, crunches, machine weights, etc.)

Today's Focus: Upper Body ☐ **Lower Body** ☐ **Abs** ☐

Muscle Group	Action or Equipment	SET 1 Reps Wt.	SET 2 Reps Wt.	SET 3 Reps Wt.	SET 4 Reps Wt.	Ease 1-10

COMMENTS: (Problems or injuries, overall mood, best/worst moment, etc.)

Other Exercise (outside the gym)

Activity	Hrs./Min./Qty.	Intensity	Cal. Burn
		Low Med. High	

Dietary Notes	CALORIES	FAT GMS	CARBS	PROTEIN
Breakfast				
Snack				
Lunch				
Snack				
Dinner				
Snack				
GRAND TOTALS...				

Water (8 oz. glasses)

☐ ☐ ☐ ☐ ☐
☐ ☐ ☐ ☐ ☐

Vitamins, Supplements

NAME / STRENGTH   QTY.

_____

_____

_____

_____

_____

_____

_____

_____

OTHER NOTES:

Met today's goals?

0%   25%   50%   75%   100%

	Week #	
Date	Day #	Day of the Week

Cardio Workout (in the gym)

		Min.	Pace/ setting	Heart rate	Cal. burn
Time of Day:	☐ Aerobics Class				
start / finish	☐ Elliptical Trainer				
Stretching / Warmup	☐ Rowing Machine				
YES___ NO___	☐ Stair Climber				
Trainer/Instructor:	☐ Stationary Bike				
	☐ Treadmill				
Exercise Buddy:					

Strength Training (Free weights, crunches, machine weights, etc.)

Today's Focus: Upper Body ☐ **Lower Body** ☐ **Abs** ☐

Muscle Group	Action or Equipment	SET 1 Reps Wt.	SET 2 Reps Wt.	SET 3 Reps Wt.	SET 4 Reps Wt.	Ease 1-10

COMMENTS: (Problems or injuries, overall mood, best/worst moment, etc.)

Other Exercise (outside the gym)

Activity	Hrs./Min./Qty.	Intensity	Cal. Burn
		Low Med. High	

Dietary Notes	CALORIES	FAT GMS	CARBS	PROTEIN
Breakfast				
Snack				
Lunch				
Snack				
Dinner				
Snack				
GRAND TOTALS...				

Water (8 oz. glasses)

☐ ☐ ☐ ☐ ☐
☐ ☐ ☐ ☐ ☐

Vitamins, Supplements

NAME / STRENGTH   QTY.

_____

_____

_____

_____

_____

_____

_____

_____

OTHER NOTES:

Met today's goals?

| 0% | 25% | 50% | 75% | 100% |

Cardio Workout (in the gym)

	Min.	Pace/ setting	Heart rate	Cal. burn

Time of Day:

start / finish

Stretching / Warmup

YES___ NO___

Trainer/Instructor:

Exercise Buddy:

- ☐ Aerobics Class
- ☐ Elliptical Trainer
- ☐ Rowing Machine
- ☐ Stair Climber
- ☐ Stationary Bike
- ☐ Treadmill

Strength Training (Free weights, crunches, machine weights, etc.)

Today's Focus: Upper Body ☐ **Lower Body** ☐ **Abs** ☐

Muscle Group	Action or Equipment	SET 1 Reps Wt.	SET 2 Reps Wt.	SET 3 Reps Wt.	SET 4 Reps Wt.	Ease 1-10

COMMENTS: (Problems or injuries, overall mood, best/worst moment, etc.)

MemoryMinder Journals, Inc.©

Other Exercise (outside the gym)

Activity	Hrs./Min./Qty.	Intensity	Cal. Burn
		Low Med. High	

Dietary Notes	CALORIES	FAT GMS.	CARBS	PROTEIN
Breakfast				
Snack				
Lunch				
Snack				
Dinner				
Snack				
GRAND TOTALS...				

Water (8 oz. glasses)

☐ ☐ ☐ ☐ ☐
☐ ☐ ☐ ☐ ☐

Vitamins, Supplements

NAME / STRENGTH   QTY.

OTHER NOTES:

Met today's goals?

0%   25%   50%   75%   100%

	Week #	
Date	Day #	Day of the Week

Cardio Workout (in the gym)

	Min.	Pace/ setting	Heart rate	Cal. burn

Time of Day:	☐ Aerobics Class				
start / finish	☐ Elliptical Trainer				
Stretching / Warmup	☐ Rowing Machine				
YES___ NO___	☐ Stair Climber				
Trainer/Instructor:	☐ Stationary Bike				
	☐ Treadmill				
Exercise Buddy:					

Strength Training (Free weights, crunches, machine weights, etc.)

Today's Focus: Upper Body ☐ **Lower Body** ☐ **Abs** ☐

Muscle Group	Action or Equipment	SET 1 Reps Wt.	SET 2 Reps Wt.	SET 3 Reps Wt.	SET 4 Reps Wt.	Ease 1-10

COMMENTS: (Problems or injuries, overall mood, best/worst moment, etc.)

Other Exercise (outside the gym)

Activity	Hrs./Min./Qty.	Intensity	Cal. Burn
		Low Med. High	

Dietary Notes

Dietary Notes	CALORIES	FAT GMS	CARBS	PROTEIN
Breakfast				
Snack				
Lunch				
Snack				
Dinner				
Snack				
GRAND TOTALS...				

Water (8 oz. glasses)

☐ ☐ ☐ ☐ ☐
☐ ☐ ☐ ☐ ☐

Vitamins, Supplements

NAME / STRENGTH   QTY.

_____

_____

_____

_____

_____

_____

_____

_____

OTHER NOTES:

Met today's goals?

| 0% | 25% | 50% | 75% | 100% |

Date	Week #	
	Day #	Day of the Week

Cardio Workout (in the gym)

		Min.	Pace/ setting	Heart rate	Cal. burn
Time of Day: start / finish	☐ Aerobics Class				
	☐ Elliptical Trainer				
Stretching / Warmup YES___ NO___	☐ Rowing Machine				
	☐ Stair Climber				
Trainer/Instructor:	☐ Stationary Bike				
	☐ Treadmill				
Exercise Buddy:					

Strength Training (Free weights, crunches, machine weights, etc.)

Today's Focus: Upper Body ☐   **Lower Body** ☐   **Abs** ☐

Muscle Group	Action or Equipment	SET 1 Reps Wt.	SET 2 Reps Wt.	SET 3 Reps Wt.	SET 4 Reps Wt.	Ease 1-10

COMMENTS: (Problems or injuries, overall mood, best/worst moment, etc.)

Other Exercise (outside the gym)

Activity	Hrs./Min./Qty.	Intensity	Cal. Burn
		Low Med. High	

Dietary Notes	CALORIES	FAT GMS	CARBS	PROTEIN
Breakfast				
Snack				
Lunch				
Snack				
Dinner				
Snack				
GRAND TOTALS...				

Water (8 oz. glasses)

☐ ☐ ☐ ☐ ☐
☐ ☐ ☐ ☐ ☐

Vitamins, Supplements

NAME / STRENGTH   QTY.

_____

_____

_____

_____

_____

_____

_____

_____

OTHER NOTES:

Met today's goals?

0%   25%   50%   75%   100%

Date	Week #	
	Day #	Day of the Week

Cardio Workout (in the gym)

		Min.	Pace/ setting	Heart rate	Cal. burn
Time of Day: start / finish	☐ Aerobics Class				
	☐ Elliptical Trainer				
Stretching / Warmup YES___ NO___	☐ Rowing Machine				
	☐ Stair Climber				
Trainer/Instructor:	☐ Stationary Bike				
	☐ Treadmill				
Exercise Buddy:					

Strength Training (Free weights, crunches, machine weights, etc.)

Today's Focus: Upper Body ☐   Lower Body ☐   Abs ☐

Muscle Group	Action or Equipment	SET 1 Reps Wt.	SET 2 Reps Wt.	SET 3 Reps Wt.	SET 4 Reps Wt.	Ease 1-10

COMMENTS: (Problems or injuries, overall mood, best/worst moment, etc.)

Other Exercise (outside the gym)

Activity	Hrs./Min./Qty.	Intensity	Cal. Burn
		Low Med. High	

Dietary Notes	CALORIES	FAT GMS	CARBS	PROTEIN
Breakfast				
Snack				
Lunch				
Snack				
Dinner				
Snack				
GRAND TOTALS...				

Water (8 oz. glasses)

☐ ☐ ☐ ☐ ☐
☐ ☐ ☐ ☐ ☐

Vitamins, Supplements

NAME / STRENGTH   QTY.

_____

_____

_____

_____

_____

_____

_____

OTHER NOTES:

Met today's goals?

0%   25%   50%   75%   100%

MemoryMinder Journals, Inc.©

	Week #	
Date	Day #	Day of the Week

Cardio Workout (in the gym)

		Min.	Pace/ setting	Heart rate	Cal. burn

Time of Day:
start / finish

Stretching / Warmup
YES___ NO___

Trainer/Instructor:

Exercise Buddy:

- ☐ Aerobics Class
- ☐ Elliptical Trainer
- ☐ Rowing Machine
- ☐ Stair Climber
- ☐ Stationary Bike
- ☐ Treadmill

Strength Training (Free weights, crunches, machine weights, etc.)

Today's Focus: Upper Body ☐   **Lower Body** ☐   **Abs** ☐

Muscle Group	Action or Equipment	SET 1 Reps Wt.	SET 2 Reps Wt.	SET 3 Reps Wt.	SET 4 Reps Wt.	Ease 1-10

COMMENTS: (Problems or injuries, overall mood, best/worst moment, etc.)

Other Exercise (outside the gym)

Activity	Hrs./Min./Qty.	Intensity	Cal. Burn
		Low Med. High	

Dietary Notes	CALORIES	FAT GMS	CARBS	PROTEIN
Breakfast				
Snack				
Lunch				
Snack				
Dinner				
Snack				
GRAND TOTALS...				

Water (8 oz. glasses)

☐ ☐ ☐ ☐ ☐
☐ ☐ ☐ ☐ ☐

Vitamins, Supplements

NAME / STRENGTH   QTY.

_____

_____

_____

_____

_____

_____

_____

OTHER NOTES:

Met today's goals?

0%   25%   50%   75%   100%

MemoryMinder Journals, Inc. ©

Cardio Workout (in the gym)

		Min.	Pace/ setting	Heart rate	Cal. burn
Time of Day: start ╱ finish	☐ Aerobics Class				
	☐ Elliptical Trainer				
Stretching / Warmup YES___ NO___	☐ Rowing Machine				
	☐ Stair Climber				
Trainer/Instructor:	☐ Stationary Bike				
	☐ Treadmill				
Exercise Buddy:					

Strength Training (Free weights, crunches, machine weights, etc.)

Today's Focus: Upper Body ☐   Lower Body ☐   Abs ☐

Muscle Group	Action or Equipment	SET 1 Reps Wt.	SET 2 Reps Wt.	SET 3 Reps Wt.	SET 4 Reps Wt.	Ease 1-10

COMMENTS: (Problems or injuries, overall mood, best/worst moment, etc.)

Other Exercise (outside the gym)

Activity	Hrs./Min./Qty.	Intensity	Cal. Burn
		Low Med. High	

Dietary Notes	CALORIES	FAT GMS	CARBS	PROTEIN
Breakfast				
Snack				
Lunch				
Snack				
Dinner				
Snack				
GRAND TOTALS...				

Water (8 oz. glasses)

☐ ☐ ☐ ☐ ☐
☐ ☐ ☐ ☐ ☐

Vitamins, Supplements

NAME / STRENGTH   QTY.

_____
_____
_____
_____
_____
_____
_____
_____

OTHER NOTES:

Met today's goals?

0% 25% 50% 75% 100%

	Week #	
_____ Date	Day #	_____ Day of the Week

Cardio Workout (in the gym)

		Min.	Pace/ setting	Heart rate	Cal. burn

Time of Day:	☐ Aerobics Class				
start / finish	☐ Elliptical Trainer				
Stretching / Warmup	☐ Rowing Machine				
YES___ NO___	☐ Stair Climber				
Trainer/Instructor:	☐ Stationary Bike				
	☐ Treadmill				
Exercise Buddy:					

Strength Training (Free weights, crunches, machine weights, etc.)

Today's Focus: Upper Body ☐ **Lower Body** ☐ **Abs** ☐

Muscle Group	Action or Equipment	SET 1 Reps Wt.	SET 2 Reps Wt.	SET 3 Reps Wt.	SET 4 Reps Wt.	Ease 1-10

COMMENTS: (Problems or injuries, overall mood, best/worst moment, etc.)

Other Exercise (outside the gym)

Activity	Hrs./Min./Qty.	Intensity	Cal. Burn
		Low Med. High	

Dietary Notes	CALORIES	FAT GMS.	CARBS	PROTEIN
Breakfast				
Snack				
Lunch				
Snack				
Dinner				
Snack				
GRAND TOTALS...				

Water (8 oz. glasses)

☐ ☐ ☐ ☐ ☐
☐ ☐ ☐ ☐ ☐

Vitamins, Supplements

NAME / STRENGTH   QTY.

OTHER NOTES:

Met today's goals?

0%   25%   50%   75%   100%

Date	Week #	
	Day #	Day of the Week

Cardio Workout (in the gym)

	Min.	Pace/ setting	Heart rate	Cal. burn

Time of Day:

start / finish

Stretching / Warmup

YES___ NO___

Trainer/Instructor:

Exercise Buddy:

	Min.	Pace/ setting	Heart rate	Cal. burn
☐ Aerobics Class				
☐ Elliptical Trainer				
☐ Rowing Machine				
☐ Stair Climber				
☐ Stationary Bike				
☐ Treadmill				

Strength Training (Free weights, crunches, machine weights, etc.)

Today's Focus: Upper Body ☐   Lower Body ☐   Abs ☐

Muscle Group	Action or Equipment	SET 1 Reps Wt.	SET 2 Reps Wt.	SET 3 Reps Wt.	SET 4 Reps Wt.	Ease 1-10

COMMENTS: (Problems or injuries, overall mood, best/worst moment, etc.)

Other Exercise (outside the gym)

Activity	Hrs./Min./Qty.	Intensity	Cal. Burn
		Low Med. High	

Dietary Notes	CALORIES	FAT GMS.	CARBS	PROTEIN
Breakfast				
Snack				
Lunch				
Snack				
Dinner				
Snack				
GRAND TOTALS...				

Water (8 oz. glasses)

☐ ☐ ☐ ☐ ☐
☐ ☐ ☐ ☐ ☐

Vitamins, Supplements

NAME / STRENGTH   QTY.

OTHER NOTES:

Met today's goals?

0%   25%   50%   75%   100%

	Week #	
Date	Day #	Day of the Week

Cardio Workout (in the gym)

		Min.	Pace/ setting	Heart rate	Cal. burn

Time of Day:	☐ Aerobics Class				
start / finish	☐ Elliptical Trainer				
Stretching / Warmup	☐ Rowing Machine				
YES___ NO___	☐ Stair Climber				
Trainer/Instructor:	☐ Stationary Bike				
	☐ Treadmill				
Exercise Buddy:					

Strength Training (Free weights, crunches, machine weights, etc.)

Today's Focus: Upper Body ☐   **Lower Body** ☐   **Abs** ☐

Muscle Group	Action or Equipment	SET 1 Reps Wt.	SET 2 Reps Wt.	SET 3 Reps Wt.	SET 4 Reps Wt.	Ease 1-10

COMMENTS: (Problems or injuries, overall mood, best/worst moment, etc.)

Other Exercise (outside the gym)

Activity	Hrs./Min./Qty.	Intensity	Cal. Burn
		Low Med. High	

Dietary Notes	CALORIES	FAT GMS	CARBS	PROTEIN
Breakfast				
Snack				
Lunch				
Snack				
Dinner				
Snack				
GRAND TOTALS...				

Water (8 oz. glasses)

☐ ☐ ☐ ☐ ☐
☐ ☐ ☐ ☐ ☐

Vitamins, Supplements

NAME / STRENGTH   QTY.

_____

_____

_____

_____

_____

_____

_____

_____

OTHER NOTES:

Met today's goals?

0%   25%   50%   75%   100%

	Week #	
Date	Day #	Day of the Week

Cardio Workout (in the gym)

		Min.	Pace/ setting	Heart rate	Cal. burn
Time of Day:	☐ Aerobics Class				
start / finish	☐ Elliptical Trainer				
Stretching / Warmup	☐ Rowing Machine				
YES___ NO___	☐ Stair Climber				
Trainer/Instructor:	☐ Stationary Bike				
	☐ Treadmill				
Exercise Buddy:					

Strength Training (Free weights, crunches, machine weights, etc.)

Today's Focus: **Upper Body** ☐ **Lower Body** ☐ **Abs** ☐

Muscle Group	Action or Equipment	SET 1 Reps Wt.	SET 2 Reps Wt.	SET 3 Reps Wt.	SET 4 Reps Wt.	Ease 1-10

COMMENTS: (Problems or injuries, overall mood, best/worst moment, etc.)

Other Exercise (outside the gym)

Activity	Hrs./Min./Qty.	Intensity	Cal. Burn
		Low Med. High	

Dietary Notes	CALORIES	FAT GMS	CARBS	PROTEIN
Breakfast				
Snack				
Lunch				
Snack				
Dinner				
Snack				
GRAND TOTALS...				

Water (8 oz. glasses)

☐ ☐ ☐ ☐ ☐
☐ ☐ ☐ ☐ ☐

Vitamins, Supplements

NAME / STRENGTH   QTY.

_____

_____

_____

_____

_____

_____

_____

OTHER NOTES:

Met today's goals?

0%   25%   50%   75%   100%

	Week #	
Date	Day #	Day of the Week

Cardio Workout (in the gym)

		Min.	Pace/ setting	Heart rate	Cal. burn
Time of Day:	☐ Aerobics Class				
start / finish	☐ Elliptical Trainer				
Stretching / Warmup	☐ Rowing Machine				
YES___ NO___	☐ Stair Climber				
Trainer/Instructor:	☐ Stationary Bike				
	☐ Treadmill				
Exercise Buddy:					

Strength Training (Free weights, crunches, machine weights, etc.)

Today's Focus: Upper Body ☐ **Lower Body** ☐ **Abs** ☐

Muscle Group	Action or Equipment	SET 1 Reps	Wt.	SET 2 Reps	Wt.	SET 3 Reps	Wt.	SET 4 Reps	Wt.	Ease 1-10

COMMENTS: (Problems or injuries, overall mood, best/worst moment, etc.)

Other Exercise (outside the gym)

Activity	Hrs./Min./Qty.	Intensity	Cal. Burn
		Low　Med.　High	

Dietary Notes	CALORIES	FAT GMS	CARBS	PROTEIN
Breakfast				
Snack				
Lunch				
Snack				
Dinner				
Snack				
GRAND TOTALS...				

Water (8 oz. glasses)

☐ ☐ ☐ ☐ ☐
☐ ☐ ☐ ☐ ☐

Vitamins, Supplements

NAME / STRENGTH   QTY.

_____
_____
_____
_____
_____
_____
_____
_____

OTHER NOTES:

Met today's goals?

0%   25%   50%   75%   100%

MemoryMinder Journals, Inc. ©

Date	Week #	
	Day #	Day of the Week

Cardio Workout (in the gym)

		Min.	Pace/ setting	Heart rate	Cal. burn
	☐ Aerobics Class				
	☐ Elliptical Trainer				
	☐ Rowing Machine				
	☐ Stair Climber				
	☐ Stationary Bike				
	☐ Treadmill				

Time of Day:

start _____ / _____ finish

Stretching / Warmup

YES___   NO___

Trainer/Instructor:

Exercise Buddy:

Strength Training (Free weights, crunches, machine weights, etc.)

Today's Focus: Upper Body ☐   Lower Body ☐   Abs ☐

Muscle Group	Action or Equipment	SET 1 Reps Wt.	SET 2 Reps Wt.	SET 3 Reps Wt.	SET 4 Reps Wt.	Ease 1-10

COMMENTS: (Problems or injuries, overall mood, best/worst moment, etc.)

Other Exercise (outside the gym)

Activity	Hrs./Min./Qty.	Intensity	Cal. Burn
		Low Med. High	

Dietary Notes	CALORIES	FAT GMS	CARBS	PROTEIN
Breakfast				
Snack				
Lunch				
Snack				
Dinner				
Snack				
GRAND TOTALS...				

Water (8 oz. glasses)

Vitamins, Supplements
NAME / STRENGTH   QTY.

OTHER NOTES:

Met today's goals?

0%   25%   50%   75%   100%

	Week #	
Date	Day #	Day of the Week

Cardio Workout (in the gym)

	Min.	Pace/ setting	Heart rate	Cal. burn

Time of Day:

start / finish

Stretching / Warmup

YES___   NO___

Trainer/Instructor:

Exercise Buddy:

	Min.	Pace/setting	Heart rate	Cal. burn
☐ Aerobics Class				
☐ Elliptical Trainer				
☐ Rowing Machine				
☐ Stair Climber				
☐ Stationary Bike				
☐ Treadmill				

Strength Training (Free weights, crunches, machine weights, etc.)

Today's Focus: Upper Body ☐   Lower Body ☐   Abs ☐

Muscle Group	Action or Equipment	SET 1 Reps Wt.	SET 2 Reps Wt.	SET 3 Reps Wt.	SET 4 Reps Wt.	Ease 1-10

COMMENTS: (Problems or injuries, overall mood, best/worst moment, etc.)

Other Exercise (outside the gym)

Activity	Hrs./Min./Qty.	Intensity	Cal. Burn
		Low Med. High	

Dietary Notes	CALORIES	FAT GMS	CARBS	PROTEIN
Breakfast				
Snack				
Lunch				
Snack				
Dinner				
Snack				
GRAND TOTALS...				

Water (8 oz. glasses)

☐ ☐ ☐ ☐ ☐
☐ ☐ ☐ ☐ ☐

Vitamins, Supplements

NAME / STRENGTH   QTY.

_____
_____
_____
_____
_____
_____
_____

OTHER NOTES:

Met today's goals?

| 0% | 25% | 50% | 75% | 100% |

MemoryMinder Journals, Inc. ©

	Week #	
Date	Day #	Day of the Week

Cardio Workout (in the gym)

		Min.	Pace/ setting	Heart rate	Cal. burn
Time of Day: start / finish	☐ Aerobics Class				
	☐ Elliptical Trainer				
Stretching / Warmup YES___ NO___	☐ Rowing Machine				
	☐ Stair Climber				
Trainer/Instructor:	☐ Stationary Bike				
	☐ Treadmill				
Exercise Buddy:					

Strength Training (Free weights, crunches, machine weights, etc.)

Today's Focus: Upper Body ☐ Lower Body ☐ Abs ☐

Muscle Group	Action or Equipment	SET 1 Reps Wt.	SET 2 Reps Wt.	SET 3 Reps Wt.	SET 4 Reps Wt.	Ease 1-10

COMMENTS: (Problems or injuries, overall mood, best/worst moment, etc.)

MemoryMinder Journals, Inc.©

Other Exercise (outside the gym)

Activity	Hrs./Min./Qty.	Intensity	Cal. Burn
		Low Med. High	

Dietary Notes	CALORIES	FAT GMS	CARBS	PROTEIN
Breakfast				
Snack				
Lunch				
Snack				
Dinner				
Snack				
GRAND TOTALS...				

Water (8 oz. glasses)

☐ ☐ ☐ ☐ ☐
☐ ☐ ☐ ☐ ☐

Vitamins, Supplements
NAME / STRENGTH   QTY.

_____

_____

_____

_____

_____

_____

_____

OTHER NOTES:

Met today's goals?

0%   25%   50%   75%   100%

Cardio Workout (in the gym)

	Min.	Pace/ setting	Heart rate	Cal. burn
☐ Aerobics Class				
☐ Elliptical Trainer				
☐ Rowing Machine				
☐ Stair Climber				
☐ Stationary Bike				
☐ Treadmill				

Time of Day:

start / finish

Stretching / Warmup

YES___ NO___

Trainer/Instructor:

Exercise Buddy:

Strength Training (Free weights, crunches, machine weights, etc.)

Today's Focus: Upper Body ☐ Lower Body ☐ Abs ☐

Muscle Group	Action or Equipment	SET 1 Reps Wt.	SET 2 Reps Wt.	SET 3 Reps Wt.	SET 4 Reps Wt.	Ease 1-10

COMMENTS: (Problems or injuries, overall mood, best/worst moment, etc.)

Other Exercise (outside the gym)

Activity	Hrs./Min./Qty.	Intensity	Cal. Burn
		Low Med. High	

Dietary Notes	CALORIES	FAT GMS	CARBS	PROTEIN
Breakfast				
Snack				
Lunch				
Snack				
Dinner				
Snack				
GRAND TOTALS...				

Water (8 oz. glasses)

☐ ☐ ☐ ☐ ☐
☐ ☐ ☐ ☐ ☐

Vitamins, Supplements

NAME / STRENGTH   QTY.

OTHER NOTES:

Met today's goals?

0%   25%   50%   75%   100%

MemoryMinder Journals, Inc. ©

	Week #	
Date	Day #	Day of the Week

Cardio Workout (in the gym)

Time of Day:		Min.	Pace/ setting	Heart rate	Cal. burn
start / finish	☐ Aerobics Class				
Stretching / Warmup	☐ Elliptical Trainer				
YES___ NO___	☐ Rowing Machine				
	☐ Stair Climber				
Trainer/Instructor:	☐ Stationary Bike				
	☐ Treadmill				
Exercise Buddy:					

Strength Training (Free weights, crunches, machine weights, etc.)

Today's Focus: Upper Body ☐   **Lower Body** ☐   **Abs** ☐

Muscle Group	Action or Equipment	SET 1 Reps Wt.	SET 2 Reps Wt.	SET 3 Reps Wt.	SET 4 Reps Wt.	Ease 1-10

COMMENTS: (Problems or injuries, overall mood, best/worst moment, etc.)

Other Exercise (outside the gym)

Activity	Hrs./Min./Qty.	Intensity	Cal. Burn
		Low Med. High	

Dietary Notes	CALORIES	FAT GMS	CARBS	PROTEIN
Breakfast				
Snack				
Lunch				
Snack				
Dinner				
Snack				
GRAND TOTALS...				

Water (8 oz. glasses)

☐ ☐ ☐ ☐ ☐
☐ ☐ ☐ ☐ ☐

Vitamins, Supplements

NAME / STRENGTH   QTY.

OTHER NOTES:

Met today's goals?

0%	25%	50%	75%	100%

MemoryMinder Journals, Inc. ©

	Week #	
Date	Day #	Day of the Week

Cardio Workout (in the gym)

		Min.	Pace/ setting	Heart rate	Cal. burn
Time of Day:	☐ Aerobics Class				
start / finish	☐ Elliptical Trainer				
Stretching / Warmup	☐ Rowing Machine				
YES___ NO___	☐ Stair Climber				
Trainer/Instructor:	☐ Stationary Bike				
	☐ Treadmill				
Exercise Buddy:					

Strength Training (Free weights, crunches, machine weights, etc.)

Today's Focus: Upper Body ☐ **Lower Body** ☐ **Abs** ☐

Muscle Group	Action or Equipment	SET 1 Reps Wt.	SET 2 Reps Wt.	SET 3 Reps Wt.	SET 4 Reps Wt.	Ease 1-10

COMMENTS: (Problems or injuries, overall mood, best/worst moment, etc.)

MemoryMinder Journals, Inc.©

Other Exercise (outside the gym)

Activity	Hrs./Min./Qty.	Intensity	Cal. Burn
		Low Med. High	

Dietary Notes	CALORIES	FAT GMS	CARBS	PROTEIN
Breakfast				
Snack				
Lunch				
Snack				
Dinner				
Snack				
GRAND TOTALS...				

Water (8 oz. glasses)

☐ ☐ ☐ ☐ ☐
☐ ☐ ☐ ☐ ☐

Vitamins, Supplements

NAME / STRENGTH   QTY.

_____

_____

_____

_____

_____

_____

_____

_____

OTHER NOTES:

Met today's goals?

0%   25%   50%   75%   100%

Date	Week #	
	Day #	Day of the Week

Cardio Workout (in the gym)

		Min.	Pace/ setting	Heart rate	Cal. burn

Time of Day:

start / finish

Stretching / Warmup

YES___   NO___

Trainer/Instructor:

Exercise Buddy:

	Min.	Pace/ setting	Heart rate	Cal. burn
☐ Aerobics Class				
☐ Elliptical Trainer				
☐ Rowing Machine				
☐ Stair Climber				
☐ Stationary Bike				
☐ Treadmill				

Strength Training (Free weights, crunches, machine weights, etc.)

Today's Focus: Upper Body ☐ **Lower Body** ☐ **Abs** ☐

Muscle Group	Action or Equipment	SET 1 Reps Wt.	SET 2 Reps Wt.	SET 3 Reps Wt.	SET 4 Reps Wt.	Ease 1-10

COMMENTS: (Problems or injuries, overall mood, best/worst moment, etc.)

Other Exercise (outside the gym)

Activity	Hrs./Min./Qty.	Intensity	Cal. Burn
		Low Med. High	

Dietary Notes	CALORIES	FAT GMS.	CARBS	PROTEIN
Breakfast				
Snack				
Lunch				
Snack				
Dinner				
Snack				
GRAND TOTALS...				

Water (8 oz. glasses)

☐ ☐ ☐ ☐ ☐
☐ ☐ ☐ ☐ ☐

Vitamins, Supplements

NAME / STRENGTH   QTY.

_____

_____

_____

_____

_____

_____

_____

OTHER NOTES:

Met today's goals?

0%   25%   50%   75%   100%

Date	Week #	
	Day #	Day of the Week

Cardio Workout (in the gym)

		Min.	Pace/ setting	Heart rate	Cal. burn
Time of Day: start / finish	☐ Aerobics Class				
	☐ Elliptical Trainer				
Stretching / Warmup	☐ Rowing Machine				
YES___ NO___	☐ Stair Climber				
Trainer/Instructor:	☐ Stationary Bike				
	☐ Treadmill				
Exercise Buddy:					

Strength Training (Free weights, crunches, machine weights, etc.)

Today's Focus: Upper Body ☐ Lower Body ☐ Abs ☐

Muscle Group	Action or Equipment	SET 1 Reps Wt.	SET 2 Reps Wt.	SET 3 Reps Wt.	SET 4 Reps Wt.	Ease 1-10

COMMENTS: (Problems or injuries, overall mood, best/worst moment, etc.)

Other Exercise (outside the gym)

Activity	Hrs./Min./Qty.	Intensity	Cal. Burn
		Low Med. High	

Dietary Notes	CALORIES	FAT GMS	CARBS	PROTEIN
Breakfast				
Snack				
Lunch				
Snack				
Dinner				
Snack				
GRAND TOTALS...				

Water (8 oz. glasses)

☐ ☐ ☐ ☐ ☐
☐ ☐ ☐ ☐ ☐

Vitamins, Supplements

NAME / STRENGTH   QTY.

_____

_____

_____

_____

_____

_____

_____

_____

OTHER NOTES:

Met today's goals?

0%   25%   50%   75%   100%

Cardio Workout (in the gym)

		Min.	Pace/ setting	Heart rate	Cal. burn

Time of Day:						
start / finish	☐ Aerobics Class					
	☐ Elliptical Trainer					
Stretching / Warmup	☐ Rowing Machine					
YES___ NO___	☐ Stair Climber					
	☐ Stationary Bike					
Trainer/Instructor:	☐ Treadmill					
Exercise Buddy:						

Strength Training (Free weights, crunches, machine weights, etc.)

Today's Focus: Upper Body ☐	Lower Body ☐	Abs ☐

Muscle Group	Action or Equipment	SET 1 Reps Wt.	SET 2 Reps Wt.	SET 3 Reps Wt.	SET 4 Reps Wt.	Ease 1-10

COMMENTS: (Problems or injuries, overall mood, best/worst moment, etc.)

Other Exercise (outside the gym)

Activity	Hrs./Min./Qty.	Intensity	Cal. Burn
		Low Med. High	

Dietary Notes	CALORIES	FAT GMS	CARBS	PROTEIN
Breakfast				
Snack				
Lunch				
Snack				
Dinner				
Snack				
GRAND TOTALS...				

Water (8 oz. glasses)

☐ ☐ ☐ ☐ ☐
☐ ☐ ☐ ☐ ☐

Vitamins, Supplements

NAME / STRENGTH   QTY.

_____

_____

_____

_____

_____

_____

_____

_____

OTHER NOTES:

Met today's goals?

| 0% | 25% | 50% | 75% | 100% |

Date	Week #	
	Day #	Day of the Week

Cardio Workout (in the gym)

		Min.	Pace/ setting	Heart rate	Cal. burn

Time of Day:

start / finish

Stretching / Warmup

YES___ NO___

Trainer/Instructor:

Exercise Buddy:

	Min.	Pace/ setting	Heart rate	Cal. burn
☐ Aerobics Class				
☐ Elliptical Trainer				
☐ Rowing Machine				
☐ Stair Climber				
☐ Stationary Bike				
☐ Treadmill				

Strength Training (Free weights, crunches, machine weights, etc.)

Today's Focus: Upper Body ☐ **Lower Body** ☐ **Abs** ☐

Muscle Group	Action or Equipment	SET 1 Reps Wt.	SET 2 Reps Wt.	SET 3 Reps Wt.	SET 4 Reps Wt.	Ease 1-10

COMMENTS: (Problems or injuries, overall mood, best/worst moment, etc.)

Other Exercise (outside the gym)

Activity	Hrs./Min./Qty.	Intensity	Cal. Burn
		Low Med. High	

Dietary Notes	CALORIES	FAT GMS	CARBS	PROTEIN
Breakfast				
Snack				
Lunch				
Snack				
Dinner				
Snack				
GRAND TOTALS...				

Water (8 oz. glasses)

☐ ☐ ☐ ☐ ☐
☐ ☐ ☐ ☐ ☐

Vitamins, Supplements

NAME / STRENGTH   QTY.

_____

_____

_____

_____

_____

_____

_____

OTHER NOTES:

Met today's goals?

| 0% | 25% | 50% | 75% | 100% |

Cardio Workout (in the gym)

		Min.	Pace/ setting	Heart rate	Cal. burn

Time of Day:		
start / finish	

| ☐ Aerobics Class |
| ☐ Elliptical Trainer |
| ☐ Rowing Machine |
| ☐ Stair Climber |
| ☐ Stationary Bike |
| ☐ Treadmill |

Stretching / Warmup

YES___   NO___

Trainer/Instructor:

Exercise Buddy:

Strength Training (Free weights, crunches, machine weights, etc.)

Today's Focus: Upper Body ☐   **Lower Body** ☐   **Abs** ☐

Muscle Group	Action or Equipment	SET 1 Reps Wt.	SET 2 Reps Wt.	SET 3 Reps Wt.	SET 4 Reps Wt.	Ease 1-10

COMMENTS: (Problems or injuries, overall mood, best/worst moment, etc.)

Other Exercise (outside the gym)

Activity	Hrs./Min./Qty.	Intensity	Cal. Burn
		Low Med. High	

Dietary Notes	CALORIES	FAT GMS	CARBS	PROTEIN
Breakfast				
Snack				
Lunch				
Snack				
Dinner				
Snack				
GRAND TOTALS...				

Water (8 oz. glasses)

☐ ☐ ☐ ☐ ☐
☐ ☐ ☐ ☐ ☐

Vitamins, Supplements

NAME / STRENGTH   QTY.

_____

_____

_____

_____

_____

_____

_____

_____

OTHER NOTES:

Met today's goals?

| 0% | 25% | 50% | 75% | 100% |

Cardio Workout (in the gym)

		Min.	Pace/ setting	Heart rate	Cal. burn

Time of Day:

start / finish

Stretching / Warmup

YES___ NO___

Trainer/Instructor:

Exercise Buddy:

	Min.	Pace/ setting	Heart rate	Cal. burn
☐ Aerobics Class				
☐ Elliptical Trainer				
☐ Rowing Machine				
☐ Stair Climber				
☐ Stationary Bike				
☐ Treadmill				

Strength Training (Free weights, crunches, machine weights, etc.)

Today's Focus: Upper Body ☐ **Lower Body** ☐ **Abs** ☐

Muscle Group	Action or Equipment	SET 1 Reps Wt.	SET 2 Reps Wt.	SET 3 Reps Wt.	SET 4 Reps Wt.	Ease 1-10

COMMENTS: (Problems or injuries, overall mood, best/worst moment, etc.)

Other Exercise (outside the gym)

Activity	Hrs./Min./Qty.	Intensity	Cal. Burn
		Low Med. High	

Dietary Notes	CALORIES	FAT GMS.	CARBS	PROTEIN
Breakfast				
Snack				
Lunch				
Snack				
Dinner				
Snack				
GRAND TOTALS...				

Water (8 oz. glasses)

☐ ☐ ☐ ☐ ☐
☐ ☐ ☐ ☐ ☐

Vitamins, Supplements

NAME / STRENGTH   QTY.

OTHER NOTES:

Met today's goals?

0%   25%   50%   75%   100%

Cardio Workout (in the gym)

	Min.	Pace/setting	Heart rate	Cal. burn
☐ Aerobics Class				
☐ Elliptical Trainer				
☐ Rowing Machine				
☐ Stair Climber				
☐ Stationary Bike				
☐ Treadmill				

Time of Day:

start / finish

Stretching / Warmup

YES___   NO___

Trainer/Instructor:

Exercise Buddy:

Strength Training (Free weights, crunches, machine weights, etc.)

Today's Focus: Upper Body ☐   Lower Body ☐   Abs ☐

Muscle Group	Action or Equipment	SET 1 Reps Wt.	SET 2 Reps Wt.	SET 3 Reps Wt.	SET 4 Reps Wt.	Ease 1-10

COMMENTS: (Problems or injuries, overall mood, best/worst moment, etc.)

Other Exercise (outside the gym)

Activity	Hrs./Min./Qty.	Intensity	Cal. Burn
		Low Med. High	

Dietary Notes

	CALORIES	FAT GMS.	CARBS	PROTEIN
Breakfast				
Snack				
Lunch				
Snack				
Dinner				
Snack				
GRAND TOTALS...				

Water (8 oz. glasses)

☐ ☐ ☐ ☐ ☐
☐ ☐ ☐ ☐ ☐

Vitamins, Supplements

NAME / STRENGTH   QTY.

_____

_____

_____

_____

_____

_____

_____

_____

OTHER NOTES:

Met today's goals?

0%   25%   50%   75%   100%

		Week #		
Date		Day #		Day of the Week

Cardio Workout (in the gym)

	Min.	Pace/ setting	Heart rate	Cal. burn

Time of Day:

start / finish

Stretching / Warmup

YES___   NO___

Trainer/Instructor:

Exercise Buddy:

	Min.	Pace/ setting	Heart rate	Cal. burn
☐ Aerobics Class				
☐ Elliptical Trainer				
☐ Rowing Machine				
☐ Stair Climber				
☐ Stationary Bike				
☐ Treadmill				

Strength Training (Free weights, crunches, machine weights, etc.)

Today's Focus: Upper Body ☐   **Lower Body** ☐   **Abs** ☐

Muscle Group	Action or Equipment	SET 1 Reps Wt.	SET 2 Reps Wt.	SET 3 Reps Wt.	SET 4 Reps Wt.	Ease 1-10

COMMENTS: (Problems or injuries, overall mood, best/worst moment, etc.)

Other Exercise (outside the gym)

Activity	Hrs./Min./Qty.	Intensity	Cal. Burn
		Low Med. High	

Dietary Notes

	CALORIES	FAT GMS	CARBS	PROTEIN
Breakfast				
Snack				
Lunch				
Snack				
Dinner				
Snack				
GRAND TOTALS...				

Water (8 oz. glasses)

☐ ☐ ☐ ☐ ☐
☐ ☐ ☐ ☐ ☐

Vitamins, Supplements

NAME / STRENGTH   QTY.

_____

_____

_____

_____

_____

_____

_____

OTHER NOTES:

Met today's goals?

0%	25%	50%	75%	100%

MemoryMinder Journals, Inc.©

Cardio Workout (in the gym)

		Min.	Pace/ setting	Heart rate	Cal. burn
Time of Day: start / finish	☐ Aerobics Class				
	☐ Elliptical Trainer				
Stretching / Warmup	☐ Rowing Machine				
YES___ NO___	☐ Stair Climber				
Trainer/Instructor:	☐ Stationary Bike				
	☐ Treadmill				
Exercise Buddy:					

Strength Training (Free weights, crunches, machine weights, etc.)

Today's Focus: Upper Body ☐ **Lower Body** ☐ **Abs** ☐

Muscle Group	Action or Equipment	SET 1 Reps Wt.	SET 2 Reps Wt.	SET 3 Reps Wt.	SET 4 Reps Wt.	Ease 1-10

COMMENTS: (Problems or injuries, overall mood, best/worst moment, etc.)

Other Exercise (outside the gym)

Activity	Hrs./Min./Qty.	Intensity	Cal. Burn
		Low Med. High	

Dietary Notes	CALORIES	FAT GMS	CARBS	PROTEIN
Breakfast				
Snack				
Lunch				
Snack				
Dinner				
Snack				
GRAND TOTALS...				

Water (8 oz. glasses)

☐ ☐ ☐ ☐ ☐
☐ ☐ ☐ ☐ ☐

Vitamins, Supplements

NAME / STRENGTH   QTY.

_____
_____
_____
_____
_____
_____
_____
_____
_____
_____

OTHER NOTES:

Met today's goals?

0%   25%   50%   75%   100%

Date	Week #	
	Day #	Day of the Week

Cardio Workout (in the gym)

		Min.	Pace/ setting	Heart rate	Cal. burn

Time of Day:

start / finish

Stretching / Warmup

YES___   NO___

Trainer/Instructor:

Exercise Buddy:

Cardio	Min.	Pace/ setting	Heart rate	Cal. burn
☐ Aerobics Class				
☐ Elliptical Trainer				
☐ Rowing Machine				
☐ Stair Climber				
☐ Stationary Bike				
☐ Treadmill				

Strength Training (Free weights, crunches, machine weights, etc.)

Today's Focus: Upper Body ☐   **Lower Body** ☐   **Abs** ☐

Muscle Group	Action or Equipment	SET 1 Reps Wt.	SET 2 Reps Wt.	SET 3 Reps Wt.	SET 4 Reps Wt.	Ease 1-10

COMMENTS: (Problems or injuries, overall mood, best/worst moment, etc.)

Other Exercise (outside the gym)

Activity	Hrs./Min./Qty.	Intensity	Cal. Burn
		Low Med. High	

Dietary Notes	CALORIES	FAT GMS.	CARBS	PROTEIN
Breakfast				
Snack				
Lunch				
Snack				
Dinner				
Snack				
GRAND TOTALS...				

Water (8 oz. glasses)

☐ ☐ ☐ ☐ ☐
☐ ☐ ☐ ☐ ☐

Vitamins, Supplements

NAME / STRENGTH   QTY.

_____

_____

_____

_____

_____

_____

_____

OTHER NOTES:

Met today's goals?

0%   25%   50%   75%   100%

Date	Week #	
	Day #	Day of the Week

Cardio Workout (in the gym)

	Min.	Pace/ setting	Heart rate	Cal. burn

Time of Day:

start / finish

Stretching / Warmup

YES___   NO___

Trainer/Instructor:

Exercise Buddy:

Cardio	Min.	Pace/setting	Heart rate	Cal. burn
☐ Aerobics Class				
☐ Elliptical Trainer				
☐ Rowing Machine				
☐ Stair Climber				
☐ Stationary Bike				
☐ Treadmill				

Strength Training (Free weights, crunches, machine weights, etc.)

Today's Focus: Upper Body ☐   **Lower Body** ☐   **Abs** ☐

Muscle Group	Action or Equipment	SET 1 Reps	SET 1 Wt.	SET 2 Reps	SET 2 Wt.	SET 3 Reps	SET 3 Wt.	SET 4 Reps	SET 4 Wt.	Ease 1-10

COMMENTS: (Problems or injuries, overall mood, best/worst moment, etc.)

MemoryMinder Journals, Inc.©

Other Exercise (outside the gym)

Activity	Hrs./Min./Qty.	Intensity	Cal. Burn
		Low Med. High	

Dietary Notes	CALORIES	FAT GMS	CARBS	PROTEIN
Breakfast				
Snack				
Lunch				
Snack				
Dinner				
Snack				
GRAND TOTALS...				

Water (8 oz. glasses)

☐ ☐ ☐ ☐ ☐
☐ ☐ ☐ ☐ ☐

Vitamins, Supplements

NAME / STRENGTH   QTY.

_____

_____

_____

_____

_____

_____

_____

_____

OTHER NOTES:

Met today's goals?

| 0% | 25% | 50% | 75% | 100% |

Cardio Workout (in the gym)

	Min.	Pace/ setting	Heart rate	Cal. burn

Time of Day:	☐ Aerobics Class				
start / finish	☐ Elliptical Trainer				
Stretching / Warmup	☐ Rowing Machine				
YES___ NO___	☐ Stair Climber				
Trainer/Instructor:	☐ Stationary Bike				
	☐ Treadmill				
Exercise Buddy:					

Strength Training (Free weights, crunches, machine weights, etc.)

Today's Focus: Upper Body ☐ **Lower Body** ☐ **Abs** ☐

Muscle Group	Action or Equipment	SET 1 Reps Wt.	SET 2 Reps Wt.	SET 3 Reps Wt.	SET 4 Reps Wt.	Ease 1-10

COMMENTS: (Problems or injuries, overall mood, best/worst moment, etc.)

Other Exercise (outside the gym)

Activity	Hrs./Min./Qty.	Intensity	Cal. Burn
		Low Med. High	

Dietary Notes	CALORIES	FAT GMS	CARBS	PROTEIN
Breakfast				
Snack				
Lunch				
Snack				
Dinner				
Snack				
GRAND TOTALS...				

Water (8 oz. glasses)

☐ ☐ ☐ ☐ ☐
☐ ☐ ☐ ☐ ☐

Vitamins, Supplements

NAME / STRENGTH   QTY.

_____

_____

_____

_____

_____

_____

_____

_____

OTHER NOTES:

Met today's goals?

0%   25%   50%   75%   100%

MemoryMinder Journals, Inc. ©

Date	Week #	
	Day #	Day of the Week

Cardio Workout (in the gym)

	Min.	Pace/ setting	Heart rate	Cal. burn

Time of Day:

start / finish

Stretching / Warmup

YES___ NO___

Trainer/Instructor:

Exercise Buddy:

Cardio	Min.	Pace/setting	Heart rate	Cal. burn
☐ Aerobics Class				
☐ Elliptical Trainer				
☐ Rowing Machine				
☐ Stair Climber				
☐ Stationary Bike				
☐ Treadmill				

Strength Training (Free weights, crunches, machine weights, etc.)

Today's Focus: Upper Body ☐   Lower Body ☐   Abs ☐

Muscle Group	Action or Equipment	SET 1 Reps	SET 1 Wt.	SET 2 Reps	SET 2 Wt.	SET 3 Reps	SET 3 Wt.	SET 4 Reps	SET 4 Wt.	Ease 1-10

COMMENTS: (Problems or injuries, overall mood, best/worst moment, etc.)

Other Exercise (outside the gym)

Activity	Hrs./Min./Qty.	Intensity	Cal. Burn
		Low Med. High	

Dietary Notes	CALORIES	FAT GMS	CARBS	PROTEIN
Breakfast				
Snack				
Lunch				
Snack				
Dinner				
Snack				
GRAND TOTALS...				

Water (8 oz. glasses)

☐ ☐ ☐ ☐ ☐
☐ ☐ ☐ ☐ ☐

Vitamins, Supplements

NAME / STRENGTH   QTY.

OTHER NOTES:

Met today's goals?

0%   25%   50%   75%   100%

MemoryMinder Journals, Inc. ©

	Week #	
Date	Day #	Day of the Week

Cardio Workout (in the gym)

		Min.	Pace/ setting	Heart rate	Cal. burn
	☐ Aerobics Class				
	☐ Elliptical Trainer				
	☐ Rowing Machine				
	☐ Stair Climber				
	☐ Stationary Bike				
	☐ Treadmill				

Time of Day:

start / finish

Stretching / Warmup

YES___ NO___

Trainer/Instructor:

Exercise Buddy:

Strength Training (Free weights, crunches, machine weights, etc.)

Today's Focus:	Upper Body	☐	Lower Body	☐	Abs	☐

Muscle Group	Action or Equipment	SET 1 Reps Wt.	SET 2 Reps Wt.	SET 3 Reps Wt.	SET 4 Reps Wt.	Ease 1-10

COMMENTS: (Problems or injuries, overall mood, best/worst moment, etc.)

Other Exercise (outside the gym)

Activity	Hrs./Min./Qty.	Intensity	Cal. Burn
		Low Med. High	

Dietary Notes

	CALORIES	FAT GMS	CARBS	PROTEIN
Breakfast				
Snack				
Lunch				
Snack				
Dinner				
Snack				
GRAND TOTALS...				

Water (8 oz. glasses)

☐ ☐ ☐ ☐ ☐
☐ ☐ ☐ ☐ ☐

Vitamins, Supplements

NAME / STRENGTH   QTY.

OTHER NOTES:

Met today's goals?

0%   25%   50%   75%   100%

Date	Week #	
	Day #	Day of the Week

Cardio Workout (in the gym)

	Min.	Pace/ setting	Heart rate	Cal. burn

Time of Day:

start / finish

Stretching / Warmup

YES___   NO___

Trainer/Instructor:

Exercise Buddy:

	Min.	Pace/ setting	Heart rate	Cal. burn
☐ Aerobics Class				
☐ Elliptical Trainer				
☐ Rowing Machine				
☐ Stair Climber				
☐ Stationary Bike				
☐ Treadmill				

Strength Training (Free weights, crunches, machine weights, etc.)

Today's Focus: Upper Body ☐   **Lower Body** ☐   **Abs** ☐

Muscle Group	Action or Equipment	SET 1 Reps Wt.	SET 2 Reps Wt.	SET 3 Reps Wt.	SET 4 Reps Wt.	Ease 1-10

COMMENTS: (Problems or injuries, overall mood, best/worst moment, etc.)

Other Exercise (outside the gym)

Activity	Hrs./Min./Qty.	Intensity	Cal. Burn
		Low Med. High	

Dietary Notes	CALORIES	FAT GMS.	CARBS	PROTEIN
Breakfast				
Snack				
Lunch				
Snack				
Dinner				
Snack				
GRAND TOTALS...				

Water (8 oz. glasses)

☐ ☐ ☐ ☐ ☐
☐ ☐ ☐ ☐ ☐

Vitamins, Supplements

NAME / STRENGTH   QTY.

OTHER NOTES:

Met today's goals?

0%   25%   50%   75%   100%

MemoryMinder Journals, Inc. ©

Date	Week #	
	Day #	Day of the Week

Cardio Workout (in the gym)

		Min.	Pace/ setting	Heart rate	Cal. burn
Time of Day: start / finish	☐ Aerobics Class				
	☐ Elliptical Trainer				
Stretching / Warmup	☐ Rowing Machine				
YES___ NO___	☐ Stair Climber				
Trainer/Instructor:	☐ Stationary Bike				
	☐ Treadmill				
Exercise Buddy:					

Strength Training (Free weights, crunches, machine weights, etc.)

Today's Focus: Upper Body ☐ **Lower Body** ☐ **Abs** ☐

Muscle Group	Action or Equipment	SET 1 Reps Wt.	SET 2 Reps Wt.	SET 3 Reps Wt.	SET 4 Reps Wt.	Ease 1-10

COMMENTS: (Problems or injuries, overall mood, best/worst moment, etc.)

Other Exercise (outside the gym)

Activity	Hrs./Min./Qty.	Intensity	Cal. Burn
		Low Med. High	

Dietary Notes	CALORIES	FAT GMS	CARBS	PROTEIN
Breakfast				
Snack				
Lunch				
Snack				
Dinner				
Snack				
GRAND TOTALS...				

Water (8 oz. glasses)

☐ ☐ ☐ ☐ ☐
☐ ☐ ☐ ☐ ☐

Vitamins, Supplements

NAME / STRENGTH   QTY.

_____

_____

_____

_____

_____

_____

_____

_____

OTHER NOTES:

Met today's goals?

| 0% | 25% | 50% | 75% | 100% |

MemoryMinder Journals, Inc.©

Date	Week # Day #	Day of the Week	

Cardio Workout (in the gym)

		Min.	Pace/ setting	Heart rate	Cal. burn

Time of Day:
start / finish

Stretching / Warmup
YES___ NO___

Trainer/Instructor:

Exercise Buddy:

- ☐ Aerobics Class
- ☐ Elliptical Trainer
- ☐ Rowing Machine
- ☐ Stair Climber
- ☐ Stationary Bike
- ☐ Treadmill

Strength Training (Free weights, crunches, machine weights, etc.)

Today's Focus: Upper Body ☐ **Lower Body** ☐ **Abs** ☐

Muscle Group	Action or Equipment	SET 1 Reps Wt.	SET 2 Reps Wt.	SET 3 Reps Wt.	SET 4 Reps Wt.	Ease 1-10

COMMENTS: (Problems or injuries, overall mood, best/worst moment, etc.)

Other Exercise (outside the gym)

Activity	Hrs./Min./Qty.	Intensity	Cal. Burn
		Low Med. High	

Dietary Notes

	CALORIES	FAT GMS	CARBS	PROTEIN
Breakfast				
Snack				
Lunch				
Snack				
Dinner				
Snack				
GRAND TOTALS...				

Water (8 oz. glasses)

☐ ☐ ☐ ☐ ☐
☐ ☐ ☐ ☐ ☐

Vitamins, Supplements

NAME / STRENGTH   QTY.

OTHER NOTES:

Met today's goals?

0%   25%   50%   75%   100%

Date	Week #	
	Day #	Day of the Week

Cardio Workout (in the gym)

		Min.	Pace/ setting	Heart rate	Cal. burn
☐ Aerobics Class					
☐ Elliptical Trainer					
☐ Rowing Machine					
☐ Stair Climber					
☐ Stationary Bike					
☐ Treadmill					

Time of Day:

start / finish

Stretching / Warmup

YES___   NO___

Trainer/Instructor:

Exercise Buddy:

Strength Training (Free weights, crunches, machine weights, etc.)

Today's Focus: Upper Body ☐   **Lower Body** ☐   **Abs** ☐

Muscle Group	Action or Equipment	SET 1 Reps Wt.	SET 2 Reps Wt.	SET 3 Reps Wt.	SET 4 Reps Wt.	Ease 1-10

COMMENTS: (Problems or injuries, overall mood, best/worst moment, etc.)

Other Exercise (outside the gym)

Activity	Hrs./Min./Qty.	Intensity	Cal. Burn
		Low　Med.　High	

Dietary Notes	CALORIES	FAT GMS	CARBS	PROTEIN
Breakfast				
Snack				
Lunch				
Snack				
Dinner				
Snack				
GRAND TOTALS...				

Water (8 oz. glasses)

☐ ☐ ☐ ☐ ☐
☐ ☐ ☐ ☐ ☐

Vitamins, Supplements

NAME / STRENGTH   QTY.

_____

_____

_____

_____

_____

_____

_____

_____

OTHER NOTES:

Met today's goals?

0%   25%   50%   75%   100%

MemoryMinder Journals, Inc. ©

Date	Week #	
	Day #	Day of the Week

Cardio Workout (in the gym)

	Min.	Pace/ setting	Heart rate	Cal. burn

Time of Day:

start / finish

☐ Aerobics Class

☐ Elliptical Trainer

Stretching / Warmup

YES___ NO___

☐ Rowing Machine

☐ Stair Climber

Trainer/Instructor:

☐ Stationary Bike

☐ Treadmill

Exercise Buddy:

Strength Training (Free weights, crunches, machine weights, etc.)

Today's Focus: Upper Body ☐ **Lower Body** ☐ **Abs** ☐

Muscle Group	Action or Equipment	SET 1 Reps Wt.	SET 2 Reps Wt.	SET 3 Reps Wt.	SET 4 Reps Wt.	Ease 1-10

COMMENTS: (Problems or injuries, overall mood, best/worst moment, etc.)

Other Exercise (outside the gym)

Activity	Hrs./Min./Qty.	Intensity	Cal. Burn
		Low Med. High	

Dietary Notes	CALORIES	FAT GMS.	CARBS	PROTEIN
Breakfast				
Snack				
Lunch				
Snack				
Dinner				
Snack				
GRAND TOTALS...				

Water (8 oz. glasses)

☐ ☐ ☐ ☐ ☐
☐ ☐ ☐ ☐ ☐

Vitamins, Supplements

NAME / STRENGTH   QTY.

_____

_____

_____

_____

_____

_____

_____

_____

OTHER NOTES:

Met today's goals?

| 0% | 25% | 50% | 75% | 100% |

MemoryMinder Journals, Inc. ©

Date	Week #	
	Day #	Day of the Week

Cardio Workout (in the gym)

		Min.	Pace/ setting	Heart rate	Cal. burn
Time of Day:	☐ Aerobics Class				
start / finish	☐ Elliptical Trainer				
Stretching / Warmup	☐ Rowing Machine				
YES___ NO___	☐ Stair Climber				
Trainer/Instructor:	☐ Stationary Bike				
	☐ Treadmill				
Exercise Buddy:					

Strength Training (Free weights, crunches, machine weights, etc.)

Today's Focus: Upper Body ☐	Lower Body ☐	Abs ☐

Muscle Group	Action or Equipment	SET 1 Reps Wt.	SET 2 Reps Wt.	SET 3 Reps Wt.	SET 4 Reps Wt.	Ease 1-10

COMMENTS: (Problems or injuries, overall mood, best/worst moment, etc.)

MemoryMinder Journals, Inc. ©

Other Exercise (outside the gym)

Activity	Hrs./Min./Qty.	Intensity	Cal. Burn
		Low Med. High	

Dietary Notes	CALORIES	FAT GMS	CARBS	PROTEIN
Breakfast				
Snack				
Lunch				
Snack				
Dinner				
Snack				
GRAND TOTALS...				

Water (8 oz. glasses)

☐ ☐ ☐ ☐ ☐
☐ ☐ ☐ ☐ ☐

Vitamins, Supplements

NAME / STRENGTH   QTY.

_____

_____

_____

_____

_____

_____

_____

OTHER NOTES:

Met today's goals?

0%   25%   50%   75%   100%

Cardio Workout (in the gym)

		Min.	Pace/ setting	Heart rate	Cal. burn
Time of Day:	☐ Aerobics Class				
start / finish	☐ Elliptical Trainer				
Stretching / Warmup	☐ Rowing Machine				
YES___ NO___	☐ Stair Climber				
Trainer/Instructor:	☐ Stationary Bike				
	☐ Treadmill				
Exercise Buddy:					

Strength Training (Free weights, crunches, machine weights, etc.)

Today's Focus: Upper Body ☐   **Lower Body** ☐   **Abs** ☐

Muscle Group	Action or Equipment	SET 1 Reps Wt.	SET 2 Reps Wt.	SET 3 Reps Wt.	SET 4 Reps Wt.	Ease 1-10

COMMENTS: (Problems or injuries, overall mood, best/worst moment, etc.)

Other Exercise (outside the gym)

Activity	Hrs./Min./Qty.	Intensity	Cal. Burn
		Low Med. High	

Dietary Notes	CALORIES	FAT GMS	CARBS	PROTEIN
Breakfast				
Snack				
Lunch				
Snack				
Dinner				
Snack				
GRAND TOTALS...				

Water (8 oz. glasses)

☐ ☐ ☐ ☐ ☐
☐ ☐ ☐ ☐ ☐

Vitamins, Supplements

NAME / STRENGTH   QTY.

OTHER NOTES:

Met today's goals?

0%   25%   50%   75%   100%

Date	Week #	
	Day #	Day of the Week

Cardio Workout (in the gym)

	Min.	Pace/ setting	Heart rate	Cal. burn

Time of Day:					
start / finish	☐ Aerobics Class				
Stretching / Warmup	☐ Elliptical Trainer				
YES___ NO___	☐ Rowing Machine				
	☐ Stair Climber				
Trainer/Instructor:	☐ Stationary Bike				
	☐ Treadmill				
Exercise Buddy:					

Strength Training (Free weights, crunches, machine weights, etc.)

Today's Focus: Upper Body ☐   Lower Body ☐   Abs ☐

Muscle Group	Action or Equipment	SET 1 Reps Wt.	SET 2 Reps Wt.	SET 3 Reps Wt.	SET 4 Reps Wt.	Ease 1-10

COMMENTS: (Problems or injuries, overall mood, best/worst moment, etc.)

Other Exercise (outside the gym)

Activity	Hrs./Min./Qty.	Intensity	Cal. Burn
		Low Med. High	

Dietary Notes	CALORIES	FAT GMS	CARBS	PROTEIN
Breakfast				
Snack				
Lunch				
Snack				
Dinner				
Snack				
GRAND TOTALS...				

Water (8 oz. glasses)

☐ ☐ ☐ ☐ ☐
☐ ☐ ☐ ☐ ☐

Vitamins, Supplements

NAME / STRENGTH   QTY.

_____

_____

_____

_____

_____

_____

_____

OTHER NOTES:

Met today's goals?

0%   25%   50%   75%   100%

Date	Week # Day #	Day of the Week

Cardio Workout (in the gym)

		Min.	Pace/ setting	Heart rate	Cal. burn
Time of Day: start / finish	☐ Aerobics Class				
	☐ Elliptical Trainer				
Stretching / Warmup YES___ NO___	☐ Rowing Machine				
	☐ Stair Climber				
Trainer/Instructor:	☐ Stationary Bike				
	☐ Treadmill				
Exercise Buddy:					

Strength Training (Free weights, crunches, machine weights, etc.)

Today's Focus: Upper Body ☐ **Lower Body** ☐ **Abs** ☐

Muscle Group	Action or Equipment	SET 1 Reps Wt.	SET 2 Reps Wt.	SET 3 Reps Wt.	SET 4 Reps Wt.	Ease 1-10

COMMENTS: (Problems or injuries, overall mood, best/worst moment, etc.)

Other Exercise (outside the gym)

Activity	Hrs./Min./Qty.	Intensity	Cal. Burn
		Low Med. High	

Dietary Notes	CALORIES	FAT GMS	CARBS	PROTEIN
Breakfast				
Snack				
Lunch				
Snack				
Dinner				
Snack				
GRAND TOTALS...				

Water (8 oz. glasses)

☐ ☐ ☐ ☐ ☐
☐ ☐ ☐ ☐

Vitamins, Supplements

NAME / STRENGTH   QTY.

OTHER NOTES:

Met today's goals?

0%   25%   50%   75%   100%

MemoryMinder Journals, Inc.©

Date	Week # Day #	Day of the Week

Cardio Workout (in the gym)

		Min.	Pace/ setting	Heart rate	Cal. burn
Time of Day: start / finish	☐ Aerobics Class				
	☐ Elliptical Trainer				
Stretching / Warmup YES___ NO___	☐ Rowing Machine				
	☐ Stair Climber				
Trainer/Instructor:	☐ Stationary Bike				
	☐ Treadmill				
Exercise Buddy:					

Strength Training (Free weights, crunches, machine weights, etc.)

Today's Focus: Upper Body ☐   **Lower Body** ☐   **Abs** ☐

Muscle Group	Action or Equipment	SET 1 Reps Wt.	SET 2 Reps Wt.	SET 3 Reps Wt.	SET 4 Reps Wt.	Ease 1-10

COMMENTS: (Problems or injuries, overall mood, best/worst moment, etc.)

Other Exercise (outside the gym)

Activity	Hrs./Min./Qty.	Intensity	Cal. Burn
		Low Med. High	

Dietary Notes

	CALORIES	FAT GMS	CARBS	PROTEIN
Breakfast				
Snack				
Lunch				
Snack				
Dinner				
Snack				
GRAND TOTALS...				

Water (8 oz. glasses)

☐ ☐ ☐ ☐ ☐
☐ ☐ ☐ ☐ ☐

Vitamins, Supplements

NAME / STRENGTH   QTY.

_____

_____

_____

_____

_____

_____

_____

OTHER NOTES:

Met today's goals?

0%   25%   50%   75%   100%

Memory-Minder Journals, Inc.©

Cardio Workout (in the gym)

	Min.	Pace/ setting	Heart rate	Cal. burn

Time of Day:

start / finish

Stretching / Warmup

YES___ NO___

Trainer/Instructor:

Exercise Buddy:

	Min.	Pace/setting	Heart rate	Cal. burn
☐ Aerobics Class				
☐ Elliptical Trainer				
☐ Rowing Machine				
☐ Stair Climber				
☐ Stationary Bike				
☐ Treadmill				

Strength Training (Free weights, crunches, machine weights, etc.)

Today's Focus: Upper Body ☐ **Lower Body** ☐ **Abs** ☐

Muscle Group	Action or Equipment	SET 1 Reps Wt.	SET 2 Reps Wt.	SET 3 Reps Wt.	SET 4 Reps Wt.	Ease 1-10

COMMENTS: (Problems or injuries, overall mood, best/worst moment, etc.)

Other Exercise (outside the gym)

Activity	Hrs./Min./Qty.	Intensity	Cal. Burn
		Low Med. High	

Dietary Notes	CALORIES	FAT GMS	CARBS	PROTEIN
Breakfast				
Snack				
Lunch				
Snack				
Dinner				
Snack				
GRAND TOTALS...				

Water (8 oz. glasses)

☐ ☐ ☐ ☐ ☐
☐ ☐ ☐ ☐ ☐

Vitamins, Supplements

NAME / STRENGTH   QTY.

_____

_____

_____

_____

_____

_____

_____

OTHER NOTES:

Met today's goals?

0%   25%   50%   75%   100%

Date	Week #	
	Day #	Day of the Week

Cardio Workout (in the gym)

	Min.	Pace/ setting	Heart rate	Cal. burn
☐ Aerobics Class				
☐ Elliptical Trainer				
☐ Rowing Machine				
☐ Stair Climber				
☐ Stationary Bike				
☐ Treadmill				

Time of Day:

start / finish

Stretching / Warmup

YES___   NO___

Trainer/Instructor:

Exercise Buddy:

Strength Training (Free weights, crunches, machine weights, etc.)

Today's Focus: Upper Body ☐   **Lower Body** ☐   **Abs** ☐

Muscle Group	Action or Equipment	SET 1 Reps Wt.	SET 2 Reps Wt.	SET 3 Reps Wt.	SET 4 Reps Wt.	Ease 1-10

COMMENTS: (Problems or injuries, overall mood, best/worst moment, etc.)

Other Exercise (outside the gym)

Activity	Hrs./Min./Qty.	Intensity	Cal. Burn
		Low Med. High	

Dietary Notes	CALORIES	FAT GMS	CARBS	PROTEIN
Breakfast				
Snack				
Lunch				
Snack				
Dinner				
Snack				
GRAND TOTALS...				

Water (8 oz. glasses)

☐ ☐ ☐ ☐ ☐
☐ ☐ ☐ ☐ ☐

Vitamins, Supplements
NAME / STRENGTH   QTY.

_____
_____
_____
_____
_____
_____
_____
_____

OTHER NOTES:

Met today's goals?

| 0% | 25% | 50% | 75% | 100% |

MemoryMinder Journals, Inc. ©

	Week #	
Date	Day #	Day of the Week

Cardio Workout (in the gym)

	Min.	Pace/ setting	Heart rate	Cal. burn
☐ Aerobics Class				
☐ Elliptical Trainer				
☐ Rowing Machine				
☐ Stair Climber				
☐ Stationary Bike				
☐ Treadmill				

Time of Day:

start / finish

Stretching / Warmup

YES___   NO___

Trainer/Instructor:

Exercise Buddy:

Strength Training (Free weights, crunches, machine weights, etc.)

Today's Focus: Upper Body ☐   Lower Body ☐   Abs ☐

Muscle Group	Action or Equipment	SET 1 Reps Wt.	SET 2 Reps Wt.	SET 3 Reps Wt.	SET 4 Reps Wt.	Ease 1-10

COMMENTS: (Problems or injuries, overall mood, best/worst moment, etc.)

MemoryMinder Journals, Inc.©

Other Exercise (outside the gym)

Activity	Hrs./Min./Qty.	Intensity	Cal. Burn
		Low Med. High	

Dietary Notes	CALORIES	FAT GMS	CARBS	PROTEIN
Breakfast				
Snack				
Lunch				
Snack				
Dinner				
Snack				
GRAND TOTALS...				

Water (8 oz. glasses)

☐ ☐ ☐ ☐ ☐
☐ ☐ ☐ ☐ ☐

Vitamins, Supplements

NAME / STRENGTH   QTY.

_____

_____

_____

_____

_____

_____

_____

_____

OTHER NOTES:

Met today's goals?

0%   25%   50%   75%   100%

Date	Week #	
	Day #	Day of the Week

Cardio Workout (in the gym)

	Min.	Pace/ setting	Heart rate	Cal. burn
☐ Aerobics Class				
☐ Elliptical Trainer				
☐ Rowing Machine				
☐ Stair Climber				
☐ Stationary Bike				
☐ Treadmill				

Time of Day:

start / finish

Stretching / Warmup

YES___   NO___

Trainer/Instructor:

Exercise Buddy:

Strength Training (Free weights, crunches, machine weights, etc.)

Today's Focus: Upper Body ☐   **Lower Body** ☐   **Abs** ☐

Muscle Group	Action or Equipment	SET 1 Reps Wt.	SET 2 Reps Wt.	SET 3 Reps Wt.	SET 4 Reps Wt.	Ease 1-10

COMMENTS: (Problems or injuries, overall mood, best/worst moment, etc.)

Other Exercise (outside the gym)

Activity	Hrs./Min./Qty.	Intensity	Cal. Burn
		Low Med. High	

Dietary Notes	CALORIES	FAT GMS	CARBS	PROTEIN
Breakfast				
Snack				
Lunch				
Snack				
Dinner				
Snack				
GRAND TOTALS...				

Water (8 oz. glasses)

☐ ☐ ☐ ☐ ☐
☐ ☐ ☐ ☐ ☐

Vitamins, Supplements

NAME / STRENGTH   QTY.

_____

_____

_____

_____

_____

_____

_____

_____

OTHER NOTES:

Met today's goals?

0%   25%   50%   75%   100%

	Week #	
Date	Day #	Day of the Week

Cardio Workout (in the gym)

		Min.	Pace/ setting	Heart rate	Cal. burn
Time of Day:	☐ Aerobics Class				
start / finish	☐ Elliptical Trainer				
Stretching / Warmup	☐ Rowing Machine				
YES___ NO___	☐ Stair Climber				
Trainer/Instructor:	☐ Stationary Bike				
	☐ Treadmill				
Exercise Buddy:					

Strength Training (Free weights, crunches, machine weights, etc.)

Today's Focus: Upper Body ☐ **Lower Body** ☐ **Abs** ☐

Muscle Group	Action or Equipment	SET 1 Reps Wt.	SET 2 Reps Wt.	SET 3 Reps Wt.	SET 4 Reps Wt.	Ease 1-10

COMMENTS: (Problems or injuries, overall mood, best/worst moment, etc.)

Other Exercise (outside the gym)

Activity	Hrs./Min./Qty.	Intensity	Cal. Burn
		Low Med. High	

Dietary Notes	CALORIES	FAT GMS	CARBS	PROTEIN
Breakfast				
Snack				
Lunch				
Snack				
Dinner				
Snack				
GRAND TOTALS...				

Water (8 oz. glasses)

☐ ☐ ☐ ☐ ☐
☐ ☐ ☐ ☐ ☐

Vitamins, Supplements

NAME / STRENGTH   QTY.

_____
_____
_____
_____
_____
_____
_____
_____

OTHER NOTES:

Met today's goals?

0%   25%   50%   75%   100%

MemoryMinder Journals, Inc.©

Date	Week #	
	Day #	Day of the Week

Cardio Workout (in the gym)

	Min.	Pace/ setting	Heart rate	Cal. burn
☐ Aerobics Class				
☐ Elliptical Trainer				
☐ Rowing Machine				
☐ Stair Climber				
☐ Stationary Bike				
☐ Treadmill				

Time of Day:

start / finish

Stretching / Warmup

YES___   NO___

Trainer/Instructor:

Exercise Buddy:

Strength Training (Free weights, crunches, machine weights, etc.)

Today's Focus: **Upper Body** ☐   **Lower Body** ☐   **Abs** ☐

Muscle Group	Action or Equipment	SET 1 Reps Wt.	SET 2 Reps Wt.	SET 3 Reps Wt.	SET 4 Reps Wt.	Ease 1-10

COMMENTS: (Problems or injuries, overall mood, best/worst moment, etc.)

Other Exercise (outside the gym)

Activity	Hrs./Min./Qty.	Intensity	Cal. Burn
		Low Med. High	

Dietary Notes	CALORIES	FAT GMS	CARBS	PROTEIN
Breakfast				
Snack				
Lunch				
Snack				
Dinner				
Snack				
GRAND TOTALS...				

Water (8 oz. glasses)

☐ ☐ ☐ ☐ ☐
☐ ☐ ☐ ☐ ☐

Vitamins, Supplements

NAME / STRENGTH   QTY.

OTHER NOTES:

Met today's goals?

0%   25%   50%   75%   100%

MemoryMinder Journals, Inc.©

	Week #	
Date	Day #	Day of the Week

Cardio Workout (in the gym)

	Min.	Pace/ setting	Heart rate	Cal. burn
☐ Aerobics Class				
☐ Elliptical Trainer				
☐ Rowing Machine				
☐ Stair Climber				
☐ Stationary Bike				
☐ Treadmill				

Time of Day:

start / finish

Stretching / Warmup

YES___ NO___

Trainer/Instructor:

Exercise Buddy:

Strength Training (Free weights, crunches, machine weights, etc.)

Today's Focus: Upper Body ☐ **Lower Body** ☐ **Abs** ☐

Muscle Group	Action or Equipment	SET 1 Reps Wt.	SET 2 Reps Wt.	SET 3 Reps Wt.	SET 4 Reps Wt.	Ease 1-10

COMMENTS: (Problems or injuries, overall mood, best/worst moment, etc.)

Other Exercise (outside the gym)

Activity	Hrs./Min./Qty.	Intensity	Cal. Burn
		Low Med. High	

Dietary Notes	CALORIES	FAT GMS.	CARBS	PROTEIN
Breakfast				
Snack				
Lunch				
Snack				
Dinner				
Snack				
GRAND TOTALS...				

Water (8 oz. glasses)

☐ ☐ ☐ ☐ ☐
☐ ☐ ☐ ☐ ☐

Vitamins, Supplements

NAME / STRENGTH   QTY.

OTHER NOTES:

Met today's goals?

0%   25%   50%   75%   100%

	Week #	
Date	Day #	Day of the Week

Cardio Workout (in the gym)

	Min.	Pace/setting	Heart rate	Cal. burn

Time of Day:	☐ Aerobics Class				
start / finish	☐ Elliptical Trainer				
Stretching / Warmup	☐ Rowing Machine				
YES___ NO___	☐ Stair Climber				
	☐ Stationary Bike				
Trainer/Instructor:	☐ Treadmill				
Exercise Buddy:					

Strength Training (Free weights, crunches, machine weights, etc.)

Today's Focus: Upper Body ☐   Lower Body ☐   Abs ☐

Muscle Group	Action or Equipment	SET 1 Reps Wt.	SET 2 Reps Wt.	SET 3 Reps Wt.	SET 4 Reps Wt.	Ease 1-10

COMMENTS: (Problems or injuries, overall mood, best/worst moment, etc.)

MemoryMinder Journals, Inc.©

Other Exercise (outside the gym)

Activity	Hrs./Min./Qty.	Intensity	Cal. Burn
		Low Med. High	

Dietary Notes	CALORIES	FAT GMS	CARBS	PROTEIN
Breakfast				
Snack				
Lunch				
Snack				
Dinner				
Snack				
GRAND TOTALS...				

Water (8 oz. glasses)

☐ ☐ ☐ ☐ ☐
☐ ☐ ☐ ☐ ☐

Vitamins, Supplements
NAME / STRENGTH   QTY.

OTHER NOTES:

Met today's goals?

| 0% | 25% | 50% | 75% | 100% |

MemoryMinder Journals, Inc. ©

Cardio Workout (in the gym)

		Min.	Pace/ setting	Heart rate	Cal. burn
	☐ Aerobics Class				
	☐ Elliptical Trainer				
	☐ Rowing Machine				
	☐ Stair Climber				
	☐ Stationary Bike				
	☐ Treadmill				

Time of Day:

start / finish

Stretching / Warmup

YES___   NO___

Trainer/Instructor:

Exercise Buddy:

Strength Training (Free weights, crunches, machine weights, etc.)

Today's Focus: Upper Body ☐   **Lower Body** ☐   **Abs** ☐

Muscle Group	Action or Equipment	SET 1 Reps Wt.	SET 2 Reps Wt.	SET 3 Reps Wt.	SET 4 Reps Wt.	Ease 1-10

COMMENTS: (Problems or injuries, overall mood, best/worst moment, etc.)

Other Exercise (outside the gym)

Activity	Hrs./Min./Qty.	Intensity	Cal. Burn
		Low Med. High	

Dietary Notes	CALORIES	FAT GMS	CARBS	PROTEIN
Breakfast				
Snack				
Lunch				
Snack				
Dinner				
Snack				
GRAND TOTALS...				

Water (8 oz. glasses)

☐ ☐ ☐ ☐ ☐
☐ ☐ ☐ ☐ ☐

Vitamins, Supplements
NAME / STRENGTH   QTY.

OTHER NOTES:

Met today's goals?

0%   25%   50%   75%   100%

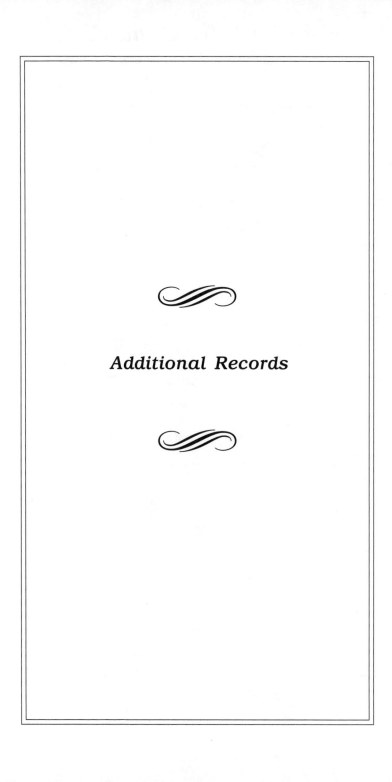

Additional Records

~Health Clubs, Gyms, Etc.~

Name of Facility_____

Address_____

_____

Phone Number _____

My Account Number_____

Fees:

Monthly: $_____, due the _____ of each month

Annual: $_____, due _____

Notes:

Name of Facility_____

Address_____

_____

Phone Number _____

My Account Number_____

Fees:

Monthly: $_____, due the _____ of each month

Annual: $_____, due _____

Notes:

Name of Facility_____

Address_____

_____

Phone Number _____

My Account Number_____

Fees:

Monthly: $_____, due the _____ of each month

Annual: $_____, due _____

Notes:

~ *Starting Stats & 13-Week Goals* ~

Start Date_____

		CURRENT	13 WEEK GOALS
EXERCISE			
Workout time...	minutes per day	_____	_____
Other exercise...	minutes per day	_____	_____
FOOD & BEVERAGES			
Calories...	per day	_____	_____
Fat...	grams per day	_____	_____
Carbs...	grams per day	_____	_____
Protein...	grams per day	_____	_____
Other_____	per day	_____	_____
MEASUREMENTS			
Height	_____ft., _____in.		
Weight...	pounds	_____	_____
Body fat...	percentage	_____%	_____%
Blood pressure...	reading	_____/___	____/___
Heart rate (resting)	beats per min.	_____	_____
Neck...	inches	_____	_____
Shoulders...	inches	_____	_____
Chest/bust...	inches	_____	_____
Waist...	inches	_____	_____
Hips...	inches	_____	_____
Upper arm (R)...	inches	_____	_____
Upper arm (L)...	inches	_____	_____
Thigh (R)...	inches	_____	_____
Thigh (L)...	inches	_____	_____
Calf (R)...	inches	_____	_____
Calf (L)...	inches	_____	_____
Other_____	inches	_____	_____
Other_____	inches	_____	_____

TO REACH MY GOALS I PLAN TO:

~*Weekly Progress*~

	Week 1	Week 2	Week 3
	Date	Date	Date
Weight			
Body fat			
Blood pressure			
Heart rate (resting)			
Neck			
Shoulders			
Chest/bust			
Waist			
Hips			
Upper arm (R)			
Upper arm (L)			
Thigh (R)			
Thigh (L)			
Calf (R)			
Calf (L)			

	Week 4	Week 5	Week 6
	Date	Date	Date
Weight			
Body fat			
Blood pressure			
Heart rate (resting)			
Neck			
Shoulders			
Chest/bust			
Waist			
Hips			
Upper arm (R)			
Upper arm (L)			
Thigh (R)			
Thigh (L)			
Calf (R)			
Calf (L)			

~*Weekly Progress*~

	Week 7	Week 8	Week 9
	Date	Date	Date
Weight			
Body fat			
Blood pressure			
Heart rate (resting)			
Neck			
Shoulders			
Chest/bust			
Waist			
Hips			
Upper arm (R)			
Upper arm (L)			
Thigh (R)			
Thigh (L)			
Calf (R)			
Calf (L)			

	Week 10	Week 11	Week 12	Week 13
	Date	Date	Date	Date
Weight				
Body fat				
Blood pressure				
Heart rate				
Neck				
Shoulders				
Chest/bust				
Waist				
Hips				
Upper arm (R)				
Upper arm (L)				
Thigh (R)				
Thigh (L)				
Calf (R)				
Calf (L)				

~Games & Competitions~

Date	Event & Location	Participants	Result/Score

~Games & Competitions~

Date	Event & Location	Participants	Result/Score

~Games & Competitions~

Date	Event & Location	Participants	Result/Score

~Games & Competitions~

Date	Event & Location	Participants	Result/Score

$ ~*Fitness Expenses*~ $

Athletic Clothing
Shoes, shorts, shirts, etc.

Date	Item	Amount Paid
		$
		$
		$
		$
		$
		$
		$
		$
		$
		$
		$
		$
		$
		$
		$

Equipment Purchases
Weights, balls, raquets, clubs, etc.

Date	Item	Amount Paid
		$
		$
		$
		$
		$
		$
		$
		$
		$
		$
		$
		$
		$
		$

$ ~*Fitness Expenses*~ $

Fees and Rentals
Membership fees, green fees, equipment rental, etc.

Date	Item	Amount Paid
		$
		$
		$
		$
		$
		$
		$
		$
		$
		$
		$
		$
		$
		$
		$

Healthfood and Miscellaneous
Vitamins, energy bars, magazines, etc.

Date	Item	Amount Paid
		$
		$
		$
		$
		$
		$
		$
		$
		$
		$
		$
		$
		$
		$
		$

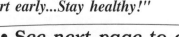

To order additional journals...

Mail this order form with your check or money order to:

MemoryMinder Journals
PO Box 23108 • Eugene, OR 97402-0425
(Please allow 1-2 weeks for delivery)
For Visa/Mastercard orders call 1(800) 888-3392 <u>or</u> (541)342-2300

For more information or quotes on large quantities,
call or visit our website,
www.memoryminder.com

SAVE!
When you order more than one, deduct $2 per journal!

- ✂ - - -

BodyMinder *Workout & Exercise Journal*

Color and Quantity: *See your goals become reality!*

Black_____   Burgundy_____   @ **$14.95** each = $_____

DietMinder *Personal Food & Fitness Journal*

Color and Quantity: *Change your eating habits for good!*

Forest Green_____   Dark Purple_____   @ **$14.95** each = $_____

HealthMinder *Personal Wellness Journal*

Color and Quantity: *Take control of your health!*

Navy_____   Red_____   @ **$14.95** each = $_____

MaintenanceMinder *Daily Weigh-In Journal*

Color and Quantity: *You took it off, now keep it off!*

Deep Brown_____   Ivory_____   @ **$16.95** each = $_____

DietMinder JUNIOR *Journal for Kids 6 & Up*

Quantity_____   *Start Early-Stay Healthy!*   @ **$10.95** each = $_____

*Discount...$2 off each book when ordering 2 or more: (minus) ($—_____)

Subtotal $_____

Shipping/Handling: add $4.95 for the first book = $____4.95_____

...plus $1.00 for each additional book = $_____

Total (Payment enclosed) = $

*Please circle where you learned about **MemoryMinder** Journals:*

Magazine   Store   Friend   Internet   Other_____

Name_____Phone (_____)_____
Required on all mail orders.

Company/organization_____

Mailing Address_____

City_____St_____Zip_____

order form

on reverse

ISBN# 978-0-9637968-4-4